Information for Management:

A Handbook

Edited by
James M. Matarazzo
and
Miriam A. Drake

Special Libraries Association

Copyright © 1994 by Special Libraries Association
1700 Eighteenth Street, N.W.
Washington, D.C. 20009-2508

All rights reserved.
Reproduction of this book, in whole or part, without written permission of the publisher is
prohibited.
Manufactured in the United States of America.
Printed on acid-free paper.

Library of Congress Cataloging-in-Publication Data

Information for management : a handbook / edited by James M. Matarazzo
  and Miriam A. Drake.
      p.   cm.
  Includes bibliographical references.
  ISBN 0-87111-427-5
  1. Corporations--Information services--Management. 2. Information
resources management. 3. Corporate libraries.   I. Matarazzo, James
M.   II. Drake, Miriam A.
HD30.35.I53 1994
027.6'9--dc20   94-21486
                                                        CIP

Contents

Introduction

Corporate libraries are being downsized, right-sized, re-engineered, outsourced, and eliminated. University administrators are looking at ways of downsizing academic libraries and reducing their costs.

SLA members have expressed fear that Information Systems in corporations and academe may make libraries obsolete. Librarians have expressed concerns about their role in the information transfer process in an electronic and networked environment. There appears to be confusion about the role of Information Systems. While there is need for collaboration between Information Systems and libraries, many librarians do not know how to work with technology people in productive way.

The business literature is full of complaints about Information Systems, its technical approach, its failure to deliver needed content and the huge amounts of money it consumes. Information Systems deals with information logistics including the transmission, receipt, storage and manipulation of data. Their expertise is in computing and telecommunications technology, not information. Technical people often do not relate to business issues or the content of people's information needs. To IS a byte is a byte. Librarians are concerned with content of the byte.

Information, knowledge, ability to learn, change and adapt and management of time are key assets today. The chapters in this book reflect the need for strategic thinking about information and the need to be adaptive and flexible. In addition, the articles stress the importance of knowing your organization's business, plans, and budgeting and planning processes.

In talking with SLA members sometimes it is not clear whether members understand the nature of the businesses in which they are employed and how information they supply is used by the people making decisions, solving problems and supporting the business. Many librarians work at the company, rather than for the company. It is not clear how many special librarians understand the information needs of their clients and users. For example, do librarians know what kinds of information senior managers want on their desks every day? How is the integration of internal and external information being accomplished? How well do librarians respond to the need for information which has been analyzed, evaluated and synthesized? Do they know the difference between raw data, information and knowledge? Are librarians responding to the context of an individual's information needs? How many librarians are providing useful content instead of access?

Success in any organization depends on contribution to productivity, achievement of objectives and the bottom line. Success also depends on knowing customers, exceeding customer expectations, using information technology appropriately and delivering useful and valuable products and services that a make a difference for the customer and the organization. Continuous feedback and measurement of customer satisfaction are essential.

Ability to communicate also is imperative. People do not speak library language. We must speak the language of the people whom we serve. Librarians in large organizations often must learn many languages ranging from physics to marketing to finance.

Many questions have been raised about SLA's support of research and SLA's research agenda. Special librarians are practical people who look for quick and useful solutions to problems. Some members have expressed doubts about SLA's investment in research because they see no direct and immediate benefit to themselves. Tobi Brimsek's chapter on the results of SLA sponsored research points out the value of research and how research results can be used by special librarians.

The topics in this book range from assessment of information needs to delivery of information on a global basis. The authors work in all types of companies and organizations and all sizes of libraries. They bring valuable experience and perspectives to their topics.

Although the book is intended primarily for corporate librarians it contains chapters that will be of interest to academic, government and other librarians. The book is not intended to be a recipe book for quick success, nor it is intended to be a text book. Its purpose is to provide strategies, techniques and methods that have worked for special librarians and their organizations. This book provides practical advice, think pieces and case studies. The book is best used as a source book for ideas, techniques, methods and successful ways of "putting knowledge to work".

I thank the authors who contributed their insights, experience, successful strategies, and time to this book. I thank David Bender for his patience, guidance and wise counsel. I deeply appreciate Jim Matarazzo's boundless energy, tireless efforts, great enthusiasm and master touch in bringing this book into reality.

Miriam A. Drake
Atlanta, GA
May 10, 1994

About the Contributors

James M. Matarazzo is professor, Graduate School of Library and Information Science, Simmons College, Boston, Massachusetts.

Miriam A. Drake is dean and director of libraries, Georgia Institute of Technology, Atlanta, Georgia and past-president of the Special Libraries Association.

Janice Davidson is senior resource specialist, and **Estelle Alexander** is acting manager, Technical Services Section — both at the Research Information Center, American Association of Retired Persons, Washington, D.C.

Kaycee Hale is executive director of the Resource and Research Center at the Fashion Institute of Design and Merchandising, Los Angeles, California.

Lou B. Parris is supervisor, Support Services, Exxon Production Company, Houston, Texas.

Susan A. Merry is director, Business Information and Records Management, Canadian Imperial Bank of Commerce, Toronto, Canada.

Beth Duston is president of Information Strategists, Manchester, New Hampshire.

Laurence Prusak is principal, Center for Information Technology and Strategy, Ernst and Young, Boston, Massachusetts.

Tobi A. Brimsek is assistant executive director, Information Services, Special Libraries Association, Washington, D.C.

Candy Schwartz is associate professor, Graduate School of Library and Information Science, Simmons College, Boston, Massachusetts.

Barbara M. Spiegelman is manager of technical information and communication, Energy Systems Business Unit, Westinghouse Electric Corporation, Pittsburgh, Pennsylvania.

Jane L. Rich is senior information resource analyst, Information Resources Group, Lotus Development Corporation, Cambridge, Massachusetts.

Monica Ertel is manager, Technology Services, Apple Computer, Cupertino, California.

Bobb Menk is senior technical librarian at Bolt Beranck and Newman, and **David Escalante** is microcomputer coordinator at Bolt Beranek & Newman, Cambridge, Massachusetts.

Michel Bauwens is editor-in-chief of *Wave* magazine, Riverland Publications, Zaventem, Belgium.

Saralyn Ingram is associate director, Information Services/Library, Consumers Union, Yonkers, New York.

Joan Gervino is director of the Center for Banking Information at the American Bankers Association, Washington, DC.

Margaret McClure is director, Information Services at KPMG Peat Marwick, Dallas, Texas.

Chapter 1
Information Management: A Process Review
James M. Matarazzo

A Process View

Many books and articles in this field have been produced to introduce us to and influence us in favor of a specific technology. Whether it is a cataloging module or a circulation system, the focus has been on the technology and not on the information. However, corporate information has many names and an equal number of access points. It is in people's heads and in their files. Information, valuable information, is often in their briefcases, phone books or on the shelves of the corporate library. Managing information requires building bridges between sources of knowledge. These knowledge sources may or may not be in the existing computer system. It is important, then, for the manager of an information resource center to be familiar with the complex world of information sources, human or otherwise.

One way to gain the needed familiarity is to use a process module. A process model is helpful in identifying the key tasks by which information is acquired, stored and used. Figure 1 is a general model of these tasks within a process perspective.[1] The sequence of presentation is logical, but it may not be necessary for the tasks to be addressed in any order. Indeed, improving any of these process tasks will have a beneficial effect on the use of information in any organization.

Figure 1
A Process Model of Information Management

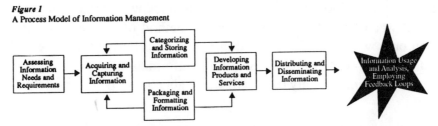

This process model links activities that are otherwise separated by functional, managerial or other boundaries. Since information management is cross functional, the expertise of others at an organization may be necessary and even desirable to produce new and more effective approaches and mechanisms to manage information.

Obviously, if the whole information management process is to be seriously studied and revised, a significant amount of resources and time will be necessary. Few firms make the opportunity available for a complete review of all of these processes. The following sections provide a review and offer approaches to their accomplishment.

Information Needs Assessment

From our own research and from years working as consultants, my colleagues and I have found that the tasks of identifying information needs is a real challenge for most information managers. As consultants, we often find information systems in place that are designed to meet expressed needs. The difficulty appears to be the tendency for changes in the business to make those needs obsolete, which should cause those systems to change. The reality is that the systems in the information center continue as if the business need is still present or is destined to return at some unknown timeframe in the future.

Many of the processes put in place to meet perceived needs today will not be sufficient to provide solutions over the long-term. Thus, systems put in place must be modular and reviewed in light of business needs in a systematic way. If not, corporate information managers will continue to add system on top of system until none is capable of being executed in a competent fashion. The focus must shift from doing things right, to doing the right things.

Information professionals have an urgent need to become fully acquainted with the business they serve and the needs of their customers within their companies. This will require the information specialist to physically leave the borders of the library and become more accessible in the organization. Only when we leave the "lair" will we be able to understand the kind of information our customers need and how it is subsequently used.

In the Summer 1992 issue of *Special Libraries*[2], Roger Jester, Manager of Management Communication at IBM's World Trade America Group, observed the following:

> I find it strange that in my two decades of experience in a major American corporation, I have yet to see corporate librarians attending a business results or product review meeting. I have attended my fair share of business strategy sessions with colleagues from practically every corporate function but I cannot recall a single instance when a member of the librarian's staff was present.

In assessing user needs, information specialists need to know customer needs firsthand. These needs come to light when customers meet. Another method of assessing customer needs is a focused discussion on how information is used in a variety of business contexts. Participants in these discussions often express the requirements for information as well as the content of the information necessary. Then, and only then, will we be able to build systems to meet the needs of our customers.

Acquiring Information

Most corporate librarians cannot afford the luxury of building collections in the same sense as their counterparts in academic institutions. Even if the funds were available, the space in most corporate information centers will not allow for the classic collection development program to be in place. Instead, corporate libraries strive to have access to the appropriate information on a continuous and systematic basis.

A colleague and I visited the Business Information Center at Toshiba in Japan.[3] One of the functions this Center provides is systematic and continuous information on subjects of high interest to the staff of the Company. Each day a great deal of information arrives at the Center from databases, government reports, journal articles, reports from staff in the field and a whole host of other sources.

A team in the Business Information Center is trusted to know which sources should be briefly abstracted, translated, and made available to the system users. All of the information is read by the staff and those stories and reports with specific meaning to the firm are added to a system, called TOSFILE. All of this work is done by a team of librarians, systems managers, and library managers who understand the firm and the needs of their internal customers.

It would be technically possible at Toshiba to distribute all of the raw data to executives and managers. However, no one would have the time to read or even scan all of the material. The significance of the service is that a human intermediary is placed between the information and the customer. These individuals at the Business Information Center have the experience and knowledge *to filter the information* for those who will ultimately use it.

A high cost, in terms of staff and expense, is associated with this information capture system. The executives at this firm, however, feel it is worth the expense to receive the best available information. The staff of the Business Information Center are trusted employees who recognize quality and the relevance of the information they scan. In light of the time constraints faced by busy staff at Toshiba, the system is appreciated and used. And, use is a key factor in any information system. At Toshiba, 30% of the staff of the Corporate Headquarters make use of the system on a daily basis.

Figure 2

Toshiba – Distributing Information Effectively

Firm's Business Information Center acquires materials and distributes information technology to 600 users daily through TOSFILE.

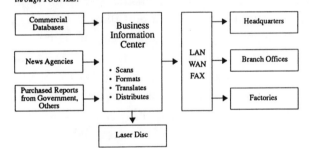

System has 600 daily users. Near-future plan calls for text and image sent by satellite to non-Japan facilities.

The technology that makes this system possible is important, to be sure, but it is secondary to the information that is sent out over the system. Bud Mathaisel, Director of Ernst & Young's Center for Information Technology and Strategy, made the point about the pre-eminent value of information when he recently wrote:

> There are clear signs that information, per se, is finally becoming a full partner with technology. In recent long-range strategic planning studies we have witnessed a familiar theme once again re-emerging — executives are stressing timely and relevant information with which to manage their businesses and this theme is rising in prominence relative to others in the planning process.

Organizing and Storing Information

It seems obvious that the only way to make appropriate decisions on how information should be organized and stored is to view these plans in the light of internal customers and the business to be served. Several basic questions must be addressed:

- What business function will be advanced by the organization and storage of the material?
- How will the customers be better served by the proposed organization and storage scheme?
- What information is to be organized and stored?
- Does the information to be stored and organized have any vocabulary that is natural?

While the questions are closely related, the answers are important to the internal customers and to the designers of the system. It is also clear that the time and effort expended to find answers to these questions will be significant. Yet, the failure to do so will lead those who plan the systems to develop practices best applied to the organization and storage of data. Our efforts instead should be directed to organizing and storing only necessary information.

Recently a leading financial services firm asked me to assist a staff team in a review of their corporate library, specifically to help analyze the team's review of library operations. This strategic and operational review provides a good example of the application of the principles just reviewed. Our task in the review was to determine the key business functions at the firm and to determine how the library's services and products should support these functions.

Our analysis of a significant amount of data gathered at the firm has considerable relevance for information organization and storage. We found that the corporate library was committed to what we described as a storage model. Under this model, the staff collected, organized and stored a great deal of material on a wide range of subjects over long timeframes "just in case" internal customers someday might need the journal, book or report. Most of this material was on paper or microfiche, making access and storage expensive in terms of labor intensity for the library staff and an unnavigable ocean of data for the internal customers. While the library was staffed for longer than the normal week, the analysts and professional staff of this financial services firm worked many more hours than was practical to staff the corporate library.

An Information Needs Assessment of the behavior of the internal customers and their information seeking patterns revealed the following:

- The internal customer's needs were clustered around a core group of documents.
- The need for these documents was continuous and users requested these materials by document code.
- These documents were frequently ordered from a third-party vendor, even though the library had a complete set.

These findings led to a reorganization of how these documents were organized and stored, with a much stronger focus on how they were actually being used. For this area, the study team recommended the following:

- Purchase the required documents on CD-ROM.
- Make one set available for use 24 hours a day and locate it in the analysts' area.
- Make the document code the key to access the document to give the internal customers not only physical access to the material, but also a simple method of retrieval.

Information Packaging

This skill focuses on the actual form in which the information is presented to the internal client. There is most certainly a substantial body of research to substantiate the claim that when information is conceived, the medium is an important part of the message. Others feel that the content of whatever is supplied is most important and that the format is not important. Regardless of your feelings on this matter, you are urged to review the information presented in the chapter by Anne W. Talcott in the *SLA President's Task Force on the Value of the Information Professional.*[4]

Briefly, Talcott describes the work of an information professional who packages information for executives. These materials are taken by busy executives in preparation for visits to other companies. The material presented, impressive in itself, is very definitely packaged for ease of use, while representing a selection of the very best information available.

Another case worthy of note was seen in a visit to the Library of Nomura Research Company in Japan. The staff of the library were frequently called upon to provide government statistical information. Since the information in Japanese Government statistical compilations was so great, the library staff decided to gather all available government statistics, organize it, and package it in the form of a rather hefty monograph. This information package is now prepared and distributed within the Company. The packaged product proved so valuable that it is now offered for sale to others outside the firm.

What was developed, formatted and packaged to meet the need of this firm has now become an information product produced entirely by the library staff. This package of information and its sale in fact produces an alignment between the Company and its sale of research and the library and its sale of information. The packaging of information also leads us to another core component for information specialists — that of developing information products and services.

Information Products and Services

If it can be done, this process task has one of the highest returns for the information professional. This is, however, a turbulent time in business and it is difficult to secure funds for any project that will not have a short-term payback to the firm, especially to the firm's bottom line. Certainly the recent research report commissioned by KPMG Peat Marwick Management Consulting in the UK, confirms the focus on the short-term profit mentality in leading firms.

In spite of this, very successful models have come about from a more process-based approach to the management of information. The reward of use is that the internal customers of the company will find these products and services valuable and this value will be acknowledged by customers of the corporate library.

An excellent illustration of a successful project took place at the Sumitomo Insurance Company in Japan. The director of the library spoke to the sales manager at the firm and convinced him that the library staff could provide real time sales assistance to salesmen in the field. Using portable computers, sales agents prior to visiting clients, extract valuable information from the staff of the company library. This sales support system has been extremely successful and now consumes more than 90% of the library staff's time.

This project was funded by the sales department after the library director took the initiative to present the plan. This suggests that it is often easier to gain support for projects that serve the needs of other units at the firm. Projects done for research and development, marketing, and sales, can be justified, especially since their benefits, if successful, will be obvious to the sponsoring unit.

The library director at Sumitomo had a second guideline he used with this project. It had been his feeling that the most important goal of his firm, the source of all that the firm stood for, and indeed its future, was sales. He felt, because he understood the business and what really mattered, that somehow he had to align the services of the library to the strategic thrust of the firm. His sales support system from the library was the method he chose.

In another case a large electronics firm's library sought to increase staff and budget, but was told repeatedly that the library would have to remain its present size and budget for the foreseeable future in the light of current budgetary restrictions. A number of the library staff in concert with the director of the library developed an alternative to growth — that of adding a second department to the library.

The staff of the library noticed that various departments they served were in need of unbiased research and analysis on various topics. Instead of contracting out for these services, a new unit of the library was contracted for the business previously outsourced. In order to do this without any increase to the library's budget, the unit pre-sold its work for one full year to internal units. The staff was hired after the work was sold.

This effort was so successful that work had to be turned away the first year. In the second year the staff was doubled as a result of the same system of pre-selling research and analysis to internal clients. By the third year of operation, the research and analysis unit staff was larger than that of the library.

It is worth noting that both the project at Sumitomo and the one at the electronics firm were initiated during difficult business cycles.

Distributing and Disseminating Information

There is a common notion that the responsibility of the information professional ends with the delivery of a service or a product to the customer's desk or PC. This implies that the nature of the delivery channel is well-known and deserves little attention. This is clearly not the case. Instead, there is a real need to build distribution channels for the products and services of corporate libraries.

In a series of research studies, a British researcher, John Blagden[5], has demonstrated repeatedly that corporate libraries and information centers share twin problems which require both attention and resolution. Blagden has found first that the services available from corporate libraries **are known to few** at each of the firms studied. My work as consultant confirms his research...too few corporate staff members are aware of the capabilities and/or services available to them from this information resource. It is no wonder, then, that at the first sign of an internal review and/or an economic down trend, corporate library staffs and budgets are reduced, often to crippling levels.

One way to build strong and high value information channels to distribute information is to create a cost structure based on the value of service or product. While this may be counter to the strong service orientation of information professionals, a charging mechanism does place a quantifiable value on the service offerings from the corporate information center.

Charging for services also creates a distribution channel based on "mutual need" and it insures a feedback mechanism, since people are more likely to comment on a service for which they have paid. If the culture of your firm allows for charging, your services will be grounded legitimately within the context of a paid transaction and more likely to be accepted by corporate management. This subject of cost justifying information dissemination leads directly to Blagden's second finding.

Blagden also discovered that what we do in information provision for our customers has real value to our firm. The issue is for us to develop some sort of method to provide the concept of value in information provision. If we fail to demonstrate value to the firm we service, our future is tenuous at best.

Employing Feedback Loops

There is *an extraordinary lack of knowledge and information surrounding information use.* A singular exception to this situation is a study completed by Joanne Marshall[6] under the financial sponsorship of the Special Libraries Association. In this study, Dr. Marshall has provided evidence that the products and services of the corporate library have an impact on its customers. Nearly 400 executives and managers in five firms indicated that the information supplied to them by the library staff: (1) made an impact on their decision-making and (2) had some impact in exploiting a new business opportunity, on deciding a course of action, or in improved client relations. In addition, these senior staff members ranked the library and library services highly as a source of information.

We do know, however, that for the institutions in her study and for the staff of these corporations, their corporate libraries make a difference. In fact, information supplied through the professional staff of the corporate library helped avoid the loss of time, the loss of funds and poor business decisions. And Marshall has provided full details so others can replicate the study.

This is exactly the kind of information needed today since all costs are carefully monitored. In today's corporation, functions that contribute will be retained; those that do not will likely lose corporate support.

It seems to me that a significant number of my colleagues believe that the application of information technology to what in the past has been done manually will solve many of the problems they face. While the library staff may be better off with these applications, no evidence has been provided to demonstrate that our customers have been better served.

The time has come to begin to prove that all we do in corporate libraries and information centers makes this unit more *effective*. If any of the possible IT applications are to really mean anything, one must absorb the messages in *Process Innovation: Redesigning Work Through People and Technology*. The advice in this book is that all of us help change the manner in which the people in organizations work.

Many IT applications result in much more expensive operations with little bottom line justification, less the supposed "status" in the organization served. Yet, the visible and invisible costs to support these technological application are very large. To these costs must be added the acknowledged cost of time and training with little evidence that information is distributed more effectively.

Most firms document success with a very narrow view of short-term profits. In the light of this we must focus our efforts on viable and visible information tasks. A process orientation to information management can provide a guide for our efforts.

References

1. The author wishes to acknowledge extensive discussions on this model with Laurence Prusak, Principal, Ernst & Young Center for Business Innovation, Boston, MA.
2. Roger E. Jester, "To the End of the Earth: Librarians and Information Management Needs," *Special Libraries*, v. 83, no. 3, 1992, p. 141.
3. For a full report on Toshiba and seven other Japanese firms see: Laurence Prusak and James M. Matarazzo, *Information Management and Japanese Success*, Washington, D.C.: Special Libraries Association, 1991.
4. Anne W. Talcott, "A Case Study in Adding Intellectual Value: the Executive Information Service," in the President's Task Force on the Value of the Information Professional, edited by James M. Matarazzo, New York: Special Libraries Association, 1987, pp. 37-44.
5. John Blagden. *Do We Really Need Libraries: An Assessment of Approaches to the Evaluation of the Performance of Libraries*. London: Clive Bingley, 1980.
6. Joanne G. Marshall, *The Impact of the Special Library on Corporate Decision Making*. Washington, D.C.: Special Libraries Association, 1993.

Chapter 2
Information for Academe
Miriam A. Drake

Librarians in academic institutions can no longer afford to function the way they did twenty years ago. Information now is viewed as an institutional resource. Emphasis has shifted from books and journals as containers of information and knowledge to the content and substance of information and knowledge. While problems of turf and territoriality will continue to prevail in academe, information is becoming an asset critical to the success of instructional, research, administrative, and service programs.

Institutions of higher education have been and will continue to be knowledge-based. Academic and research programs always have relied on knowledge, data, and information. Higher education has been in the knowledge and technology transfer business from its earliest days. Whether teachers are working with one student or many students in a classroom, they transfer, disseminate, and communicate what is known about a particular field or topic. The academic library is considered by many to be the heart of the university for good reason. The library is the place one goes to discover, explore, and learn. Today, the discovery, exploration, and learning have been made more complex and richer by electronic information, online graphics, and multimedia.

Technology has made it possible for many students and faculty members to be self-sufficient in information finding, exploration, and learning. More ways of learning are available. Students can learn calculus by reading and solving problems with paper and pencil, or they may use computer programs or hand-held computers which calculate and display graphic representations of formulas and results.

When libraries were primarily paper-based, graphics, pictures, and illustrations were difficult to find. Technology is making it easier to find information in different forms. Customer and user expectations have been raised about what is possible in terms of information access and acquisition.

Faculty, students, graduates, administrators, funders, and other stakeholders and constituents are demanding more services and accountability. Some people see the library as a wonderful storehouse and center for the discovery of new knowledge. Others see it as an anachronism or a warehouse of old books. Many university presidents and chief academic officers believe that the libraries cost too much. They naively believe that consortia and resource sharing of print materials will save money, or they believe that costs will automatically go down when everything anyone could ever want is available over the Internet.

Survival for many academic libraries will depend on successfully managing the transition from the storage of paper and film containers to a center of learning and information service. Transforming the traditional library into a customer-oriented learning and service center—where people, problem solving, and intellectual content are more important than books and physical objects—is one of the greatest challenges facing academic librarians today.

Clientele

Each library and/or information center will have to tailor services to its unique clientele. The success of these services will depend on staff knowing their customers, their interests, the content and context of their work, and how they concentrate and learn. Coupling knowledge of customers with knowledge of the intellectual resources required to keep them up-to-date and informed, provide the basic building blocks of effective and valued customer services. There is no magic recipe that librarians can follow. They must approach customer service first by understanding that it is vastly different from what they have been doing. In addition they need to enhance their knowledge and understanding skills by learning about their institution, its environment, and higher education in general.

Academic libraries serve all students, faculty, staff, and administrators. Many libraries extend services to graduates, students, and faculty from other colleges and universities and local business. This broad market can be both an asset and a burden. The asset value derives from dealing with many people with different needs, levels of expertise, and context. This diversity often requires librarians to make priorities in services for different groups. The burden is twofold: being taken for granted, and having people assume that since the library serves everyone, it must be well funded and have everything they want.

When customer concerns are paramount, each person is recognized as unique with a unique mind-set, experiences, knowledge, and approach to problem solving. Value-added information services are not mass market items. They are based on a desire to satisfy each customer. Rosabeth Moss Kanter has stated that each customer is a segment of one. Customers don't want standardization. They want services that will work for them.[1]

Knowing customers and having an operational understanding of their needs also involves knowing about how they work and how academic organizations work. Learning about the organization involves asking many questions, seeking information, and synthesizing that information to form the basis of services to customers. This paper discusses users, clients, and customers, and the information librarians need to have and use in order to function successfully in the future.

Mission

The first question in learning about information needs is, why does the institution exist? The answer is not to educate students. Most colleges and universities have more specific missions than general education. A community college may incorporate job-related training as well as senior college preparation or remedial studies in its mission. A four-year college may be focused on liberal arts with the goal of sending its graduates on to professional or graduate schools. A large university's mission will include education, research, service, and economic development. Institutions such as MIT, CAL Tech, and Georgia Tech will place greater emphasis on technological education, science, and engineering than liberal arts colleges or comprehensive universities. An urban university will have a different mission and purpose from that of a large residential university.

Research-level and doctoral degree-granting institutions need greater information infrastructure and customer service than community colleges or liberal arts colleges. Ph.D. candidates writing dissertations create huge demands on libraries for breadth and depth of information. Resource sharing of print materials among research universities provides a cost-effective method for acquiring what is needed; however, it cannot substitute for core collections or research-level collections in fields of specialization.

Strategic Plans

What is the institution trying to achieve? What is the role of research? What is the role of sports? What activities are encouraged? discouraged? The answers to some of these questions can be found in the mission statement of the institution. The mission of most colleges and universities can be found in its charter, catalogs, and strategic plans. Goals and specific objectives usually are found in the strategic plan. Some schools have one comprehensive plan for the institution; others have unit plans. The strategic plan is a key document for librarians, information specialists, and information technologists. Most plans will contain the institution's view and understanding of its environment, its strengths and weaknesses, planning assumptions, goals, objectives, strategies, and action steps. The environmental scan and assumptions offer insights into how the institution thinks about itself and its environment. For many institutions the strategic plan serves as a guide to decision-making, resource allocation, and priorities.

Culture

Every college or university has a unique culture. While there are some shared values in academe, these values usually are discipline-based and not institution-based. A college or university's culture and values are based on its age, traditions, funding sources, power structure, and stakeholders. A privately funded university is likely to have a different culture than an institution which is largely publicly funded. There are also hybrids which refer to themselves as being state-assisted rather than state-funded. Librarians need to know who supplies the money for the institution and who decides how it is spent.

Culture dictates the nature of the power structure and how funds are allocated within the institution. It is essential to understand the power structure and institutional politics. The sources of power and decision-making are an important part of the culture of the institution. Who influences decisions can be as important as who makes the decisions. Power, politics, and tradition are critical to understanding how the library will be treated and funded.

Customer Groups

Library and information services customers can be grouped by status, interests, or level of expertise. Status groups include undergraduate students, graduate students, faculty, administration, graduates, local business, and other libraries. A second classification by subject interest will vary with the variety of subjects, size of the institution, levels and types of research and degrees granted. In a small college, general classifications, such as science, humanities, arts, and social sciences, may be sufficient. In a larger university more specificity may be needed.

A third way of grouping customers and users is by level of information competence and expertise. Faculty, in particular, will have varying levels of expertise in technology and information. Some faculty will be local experts, usually in a particular field. The experts may or may not be capable in the use of information technology to find what they want. The local experts, competent in the use of information technology, will train their colleagues and want to be someone who is consulted by others. They come to the library for supplemental support and usually want to be self-sufficient in finding and evaluating information. The role of librarians is to ensure that these local experts have competencies necessary to navigate the network, find what they need, and know about all relevant sources available. Librarians can provide valuable services by being ahead of these faculty members and keeping them informed of developments regarding networking and availability of new information resources.

The detail expert is likely to be a specialist in a narrowly defined and limited aspect of a discipline. Usually, this person knows more than anyone else on campus about the literature and activities of the specialty. This person is likely to be in touch with a small number of colleagues around the world through e-mail, distribution of preprints, and conferences. Librarians usually are not consulted by the local content expert; however, librarians may want to refer people to this local expert.

Service clients will rely on librarians, information specialists, and information systems people for answers to questions, research, and analysis and synthesis of information. They respect the expertise of information professionals and trust them to do the job they need done. They want full service and usually are willing to pay for it. They do not want to be instructed on how to find information for themselves. Often they want more than citations and abstracts. They expect to receive substantive information which has been evaluated and, if desired, synthesized. Service clients place significant value on being kept up-to-date and learning about trends in their areas of interest. They do not hesitate to rely on a trusted librarian to be the "first" source for information.

When segmenting clients, customers, and users according to levels of technological expertise and information competence, it is important to know the answers to the following questions: What is the level of expertise? What is the level of information competence? Why is the client coming to the librarian? How does the client want information delivered? How much evaluation, analysis, and synthesis does the client want? What role does the client want the librarian to play? As an instructor on sources? problem solver? information finder? researcher?

Knowing what the client wants, what he or she brings to the transaction, and what results the client expects will help to ensure a successful interaction.

Segmentation by Status

In some colleges and universities it is easier to segment clients and users by status. Teams of staff members can be designated for undergraduates, graduate students, faculty, administration, graduates, local business, and others. Undergraduate needs usually are tied to the content of the curriculum, the size of classes, and teaching styles. Course catalogs, syllabi, and other documents describing the curriculum-specific course requirements and degree requirements are essential reading for the planner of undergraduate services and collections. Familiarity with course content and close working relationships with teaching faculty will increase the probability for successful undergraduate services. Some colleges and universities are requiring all undergraduates to take a freshman course in the basics of computing, campus information systems, and use of the Internet. These courses are an ideal opportunity for librarians to teach undergraduates how to use online catalogs, databases, document delivery services, and other services available on the campus network, regional networks, or the Internet.

Libraries should avoid the standard tour and traditional bibliographic instruction. Many undergraduates will not retain what they learn in these activities unless they have a specific assignment or interest at the time. If possible, undergraduates should be given instruction in finding, evaluating, synthesizing, and using information when they have a real need. Self-motivated learning usually is far more effective than forced learning.

Successful instruction in information finding and use usually is related to the student's discipline or major. Information classes related to the elements of the student's major can be invaluable for upper-class students and beginning graduate students. Librarians should work with faculty to design the modules of these courses. For example, in a management curriculum, data and information related to finance, marketing, and other core management courses will serve as a guide for the student's activities in the major.

Students do not need a library tour when a computer-based directory system can tell anyone where things are located in the library or library system. While tours are useful to some students and faculty, they are a waste of time for others.

Graduate students require a high level of customer service. Many graduate students are teaching or research assistants. Teaching assistants working in the classroom need special instruction because they often give undergraduates inaccurate information about the library and its services. If the teaching assistant does not know how to use the library's services, it is likely that her or his students will be discouraged from using the library. Research assistants doing assignments for their sponsored projects may use the library for the first time for real-world information needs. Often they find that they do not know how to access and find the information the project requires. If librarians are familiar with research programs and current research contracts, they can contribute to the success of these projects by working closely with the research assistants and ensuring that project participants have complete information in the desired form.

Graduate students need librarians most when they begin to write their dissertation proposals, do their research, and write their dissertations. Librarians working closely with graduate students can make a significant difference in the success of the student's work. A trusting and effective working relationship between graduate student and librarian will result in a better product, save time for all people involved with the dissertation, and build a lasting relationship between librarians and alumni.

Valued services for and services valued by faculty depend primarily on developing solid working relationships. Librarians need to know not only the content of the courses taught by each faculty member but also the faculty member's current research projects, future research interests, and if possible, personal interests. In addition, librarians need to understand how the faculty member likes to work with information and information resources. Some faculty members like to do all their information finding on their own. Some want librarians to find citations and abstracts. Others want librarians to find data and information, evaluate the material, and transmit the content of what is needed.

The goal of librarians with faculty members who want to do their own information finding is to provide instruction and help to make them self-sufficient. This goal can be realized through one-on-one instruction on using networks and information resources. Faculty members who want to do some of the work themselves will need librarians to direct them to sources and teach them how to use these sources. When faculty members want librarians to find information, evaluate, and synthesize it, librarians have to know the context of the request as well as the content of the request. In all cases, librarians need to know how each faculty member wants information delivered. For example, does the faculty member want a machine-readable file? a laser printed copy of an article? a summary of findings?

Many academic librarians are not familiar with the research interests of the faculty, the content of currently funded research projects, or how each faculty member likes to work with information resources. Knowledge of research and mechanisms to keep faculty up-to-date in their areas of interest can make a difference in the way faculty members regard and value the work of librarians.

Administrators are the decision-makers of a college or university. These decision-makers may be the group most neglected by college and university librarians. As a result, many administrators hire their own information specialists and wonder why they should support a unit that is doing nothing for them.

Librarians have a unique opportunity to provide significant executive and/or management information services to institutional administrators. Many administrators are trying to view all information resources as institutional resources. Others view operational data generated by administrative computing as different from the products and services of the library. Most of these clients want to integrate institutional information and external information. They may be interested in online access to a variety of data sets and information resources to help them compare their department, college, or school with peer schools or other groups. They may want information about the potential student population. They may want to compare their finances with the finances of other institutions. In general, they want information available at the desktop computer. Librarians with an understanding of executive and management information needs and information systems can work with administrative computing staff to deliver what managers need.

Librarians often have difficulty in dealing with numeric data sets because their background and education have not equipped them to deal with quantitative data. Librarians who are quantitative thinkers and are comfortable with the retrieval and manipulation of data sets and statistical analysis can be an important asset to the administration of a college or university.

Administrators who are not library customers are not likely to know about the information librarians can provide in terms of needed data, keeping people up-to-date on trends in higher education, and integrating internal and external information. In this situation librarians have to take the initiative and work with administrators to design and implement executive information systems which meet needs and provide appropriate data quickly and in the form desired by the administrator.

Segmentation by Subject

Another way of segmenting academic clients is by subject or discipline. Subject bibliographers who know the literature may or may not be appropriate to provide direct customer service. This grouping of clients requires librarians to become familiar with the content of a subject field as well as its literature. Librarians in this mode are assigned to work with faculty and graduate students in particular fields or departments. Large universities with branch libraries often produce librarians with extraordinary knowledge of a research field or academic discipline. Because of their knowledge of the discipline and their expertise in information services, they are highly valued by faculty and students. Librarians need to know the intellectual content of courses, existing research, and emerging areas of research.

A subject approach can be carried out successfully by keeping up with the current literature of the field as well as the future of the field. Many areas of science and technology are becoming both more interdisciplinary and more fragmented. Graduate students often are more aware of trends because of the vast amounts of reading they have to do for their dissertation proposals and the dissertation itself. Faculty may or may not be up-to-date on the field.

As science and technology have become more fragmented and specialized, more and more literature has become concerned with smaller areas of a field. For example, prior to 1988 articles on what we now call superconductivity were found in journals such as *Physica* or *Physica B* and *C*. Beginning in 1988 superconductivity became a separate field with new journals, such as *Physica C, Superconductivity and Superconductivity,* and *Superconductor Science & Technology.* In 1991 the *IEEE Transactions of Applied Superconductivity* began publication. Computer science and materials science are breaking into smaller subfields with their own publications.

There are also numerous examples of greater interdisciplinary activity in science, engineering, and the social sciences. Some fields, such as information science and transportation, are interdisciplinary by nature. Others, such as biotechnology, biomedicine, and social biology, are emerging. In addition, almost every field has spawned one or more journals in computer applications. The literature in these fields may be found in many publications. Librarians serving these fields need to be sure they have a complete understanding of research activities, how the field is developing, and where research is published.

Information Technology

Information technology has changed and will continue to change the ways all people access, find, evaluate, and use information. Younger people who have grown up with technology are more likely to be successful with its use for information finding and application than older people who have had to learn how to use computers and networks as adults. Acquisition of knowledge will depend more and more on information, computer, and network competencies in the future. It is essential that all students be given instruction in basic computing and information skills.

Publishing

While print publications continue to increase every year, offerings on the Internet and the information highway will increase exponentially for many years. Faculty and graduate students working in narrowly defined fields may feel they do not need librarians because they believe they can obtain what they need electronically through communication with colleagues around the world. Librarians need to be alert to information which may be missed by these groups.

In the future, scholarly journals probably will go out of print and emphasis likely will be on the article rather than the journal. It is not clear how this information will be made available, what it will cost, or how it will be priced by publishers. The future of the scholarly publishing industry is not clear. Publishing costs are relatively inelastic, and most of the costs are incurred in producing the first copy. Publishers are accustomed to estimating their costs in terms of distribution of print products and deriving their revenue through subscriptions. Electronic distribution will change both costs and revenue. Academic libraries serving large student and faculty populations may subscribe to online journals just as they subscribe to print journals. Another possibility may be to subscribe to articles in a field at a level appropriate for the library's clientele. For example, if a university has graduate programs and research in polymer chemistry, it might be more effective to subscribe to articles in that field rather than to a broader array of titles.

In some fields, however, it may be more effective for a library to buy each article as needed. Academic institutions are likely to have some combination of subscriptions and transactions. Since costs and market factors are muddy, predictions about specific models are difficult.

Librarians, faculty, and administrators in many universities are examining the process of disseminating scholarly works in the context of the emerging information highway. Some colleges and universities are giving serious consideration to publishing the output of their faculty on the Internet rather than through commercial publishers. The premise behind this activity is that faculty produce journal articles as part of their university research and give it to commercial publishers for dissemination, and then libraries have to buy it back from commercial publishers. Electronic publishing by the university would bypass the commercial sector; however, it is not clear whether this process will be efficient and cost-effective. Publishers perform a variety of activities—such as editing, layout, and marketing—that may not be performed well by universities. Since a substantial portion of the costs of publishing journals is incurred in producing the first copy, universities may not be able to afford to enter the publishing business. Other issues related to faculty publishing being distributed electronically involve refereeing, editing, the imprimatur of a recognized publisher, and the desire of faculty to control their output.

Electronic publishing also will affect the dissemination of theses and dissertations. Policies vary on copyright ownership by universities of a dissertation or thesis. In some cases, the university will copyright all work produced by students; in others, copyright may be left to the discretion of the student. If universities publish dissertations and theses electronically, the copyright policies will need to be clarified and understood by all involved.

The market for this material raises more questions. It is likely that only a small portion of dissertations or theses is widely read. Is it worth storing the material and making it readily available?

Universities also are discussing electronic dissemination of technical reports. Carnegie Mellon University and others now are distributing technical reports in computer science electronically.

Information technology will enable more effective means of accessing older materials which now are inaccessible. Scanning older materials and making them available will increase their use. Older journals, especially from the eighteenth and nineteenth centuries, are not accessible. These volumes have not been indexed and are known only to a handful of historians of science and technology. Today's students rely on databases available on networks, local computers, and CD-ROMs for their materials. If an item does not appear in a database, it does not exist for the student. This situation could result in redundancy and the students not getting all the information they need to do their work. For example, the literature on architecture and road and bridge building goes back to the eighteenth and nineteenth centuries. That literature is not available electronically and may be excluded by students and others relying exclusively on electronic resources.

Electronic libraries and information will not be implemented at the same pace on every campus. Although many large campuses are fully networked, many are not. Many small colleges and universities have no network infrastructure and are not able to take advantage of online resources. The construction of networks will require greater bandwidth than is available on many campuses. Multimedia instructional programs that enhance classroom work or supplement the classroom will become more available in the near future. Transmission of these programs around campus and the ability to receive them from national and international networks will require significant investment in the computing and network infrastructure.

Information for Librarians

Librarians need to be ahead of the faculty and administration in their knowledge of information technology and its application to information management and learning. Many colleges and universities are engaged in writing strategic plans for their institutions that include plans for building or expanding networks and the computing infrastructure. Librarians can contribute significant value to those plans by sharing their knowledge and letting colleagues know what is feasible and desirable for the campus.

In addition to strategic plans librarians should read all newsletters, press releases, college catalogs, bulletin boards, campus-wide news services, and faculty publications. By using knowledge derived from these documents librarians will be in a better position not only to provide better customer service but also to be seen as people of knowledge and power on the campus. Reading faculty publications will give librarians a broad picture of campus intellectual life and a perspective that no one else on campus will have. Reviewing faculty publications also will reveal the interests of specific faculty members. Examination of citations in faculty publications will reveal the information resources used by faculty.

Campus newspapers and meetings with student leaders will reveal concerns of students. If librarians are willing to listen, they can acquire valuable information from students. Although it may not be possible to satisfy all students' demands, it may be possible to make changes to accommodate students' needs.

Librarians will find it useful to work with focus groups of faculty, students, and administration. In these groups, librarians can learn about current needs and how different groups view their futures and the future of the library. Although customer satisfaction surveys can provide useful feedback, focus groups create an opportunity for probing and gaining greater clarification of customers' thinking.

Conclusion

Librarians can be valued and powerful people on campus. Power does not come from numbers of books or journals or the library exit count. Power is derived from other people. Librarians possess unique skills that can add value to a number of academic and intellectual processes if these are applied with imagination and creativity. Implementation of information management systems often requires collaboration with academic computing, administrative computing, and information technology staff. Information technology staff increasingly are recognizing the knowledge and skills possessed by librarians.

Information and knowledge are the economic assets of the future and primary assets for education, research, learning, administration, and economic development. Academic librarians can be leaders in the management of those assets and increase their value for the institution. Asset management, marketing, collaboration, and customer service will be the keys to success for the academic library in the future.

References

1.   Kanter, Rosabeth Moss. *Management Review*. April 1993.

Chapter 3
Assessing Information Needs:
What Do Customers Want?
Janice Davidson and Estelle Alexander

What information do staff members need to carry out their jobs? What means do they employ to get this information and how do they use it?[1] As part of its strategic planning, the Research Information Center of the American Association of Retired Persons (AARP) had been looking at ways to increase its effectiveness and visibility. Staff members gathered and shared information about the directions in which the library information field was moving, and the challenges facing special libraries. This information-sharing process highlighted a number of important topics and issues: the changing world of information management, the need for special libraries to be seen as contributing to the productivity of the organization, the limitations of traditional ways of viewing library service, and the importance of librarians' looking outside of their usual networks for strategies developed by other disciplines to attain their fair share of organizational resources. As a result of this examination, the Center resolved to redefine its role in the organization to create a vision for the future.

Several forces drove the redefinition task. Following a reorganization of the entire AARP, the Center became part of the new Research Division. This move meant not only a new place in the organizational structure, but also a new role that emphasized reaching out to a broader audience both within and outside the AARP. Also as a part of the reorganization, AARP began to expand functions at the field office level, to promote activities at the local community level, and to put increased attention on broader roles for the volunteer leaders nationwide. Thus, a significant number of staff and volunteers would be working at locations other than the headquarters office where the Center was located. What information products and services would be most effective in light of these changes? To begin to answer these questions, the Center developed a proposal calling for a project team to design a research strategy for an information needs assessment and evaluation. The leaders of this team (the Research Information Center Marketing Team) would be Center staff members; the team members would be drawn from various divisions within the AARP.

Using In-House Staff Experts

In a new way to view and use Association expertise, the Center assembled a team with staff from the Research, Membership, and Field Services divisions. These staff were selected to provide relevant expertise on marketing techniques, field office and local community operations, and the structure and activities of the volunteer leadership. Additional staff could be asked to attend specific meetings as the need for other expertise arose.

In the early stages of the project, team leaders put themselves in the client role, seeking information and expertise from other team members. This technique provided the leaders with information on how to proceed in the project planning. After extensive discussion of project goals and objectives, team members with relevant expertise proposed the use of focus groups as an initial step in assessing the information needs of Assocation staff and volunteers. The analysis of focus group data would provide the basis for the development of a written questionnaire to survey staff and selected groups of volunteers. The team leaders agreed to this approach and developed a statement of purpose reflecting this strategy:

> The Research Information Center Marketing Team will examine the information needs of the AARP staff and volunteers. This needs assessment will gather data on how the staff and volunteers obtain and use information on the job. Focus groups, both at headquarters and field offices, will provide insights into the attitudes, perceptions, and opinions of participants concerning their information needs. The analysis of the focus group data will be used to develop a questionnaire to survey a representative sample of staff and volunteers. Information from the needs assessment will provide a basis for the Research Information Center to broaden its outreach in support of the Association's goals of quality service and effective operations.

Implementing the Focus Groups

In *Focus Groups: A Guide for Marketing and Advertising Professionals*, Jane Templeton stated that a "precise definition of a focus group is hard to come by."[2] The research team's definition of a focus group was an amalgamation of definitions found in the literature: a focus group should consist of six to twelve members called together to discuss a topic of concern, for the purpose of providing information and insight about a topic. The focus group moderator would set the tone, stimulate and focus the discussion, and ensure that all participants have an opportunity to comment.

The team member's knowledge of research methods and marketing techniques was invaluable in implementing the focus group phase. The team determined the number, composition, and location of Association market segments. Five segments were selected for the study: field staff, volunteer leaders, support staff, mid-level professionals and managers, and *Modern Maturity* staff.

The team considered the options of handling the focus group project in-house or hiring an outside firm to plan and conduct the focus groups and analyze the results. Team members decided that there was enough in-house experience to conduct the groups and analyze the results effectively, and they selected one team member as the focus group moderator. The team stressed that the moderator should understand the issues to be discussed, ask probing questions, and remain neutral concerning the topics covered. Team members who worked with the field staff suggested a number of field office sites suitable for the focus group sessions, as well as a list of possible focus group participants. Representatives from each market segment were invited to participate in focus groups, to be held both at headquarters and in the field.

The team leaders knew from their reading of the literature that developing the focus group questions was a critical task. "Much of the success of the focus group depends on the quality of the questions."[3] Team leaders specified the areas the questions should cover and the sequence the questions should take. However, they relied on team expertise to refine the wording of the questions.

This process demanded careful thinking about how to elicit specific information from participants and now they might interpret questions. (The questions are given in Appendix I.)

Each focus group discussion began broadly with an initial question on attitudes toward libraries, then moved into more specific areas concerning information needs and uses, sources and methods of obtaining information, information access and delivery, and uses and perceptions of the Center. Participants were encouraged to express their thoughts about an ideal information system. The questions were pilot-tested at the first group and revisions were made to better direct the questioning route.

In all, a total of forty one staff members and sixteen volunteer leaders participated in six focus group discussions lasting about two hours each. Two sessions were held at headquarters and four in field office locations. Participants represented a cross-section of levels, jobs, and functions.

The Center team members played a central role in handling the logistics of the focus groups, coordinating such tasks as invitations and confirmations to participants, audiotaping setup, seating arrangements, name tags, and refreshments. One or two team members attended each focus group as observers and were available to answer questions about what the Center does, thus increasing the visibility of the Center's activities and services. After the session, they joined the moderator to capture and record key points and observations about the group responses.

One member, chosen by the team, analyzed the focus group information and prepared a focus group report. This task involved transcribing the audiotapes and summarizing each focus group session. To illustrate and accurately reflect the sense of each group, many quotations of participants were included in the summaries. Particular attention was given to the consistency of responses. The major ideas and trends which emerged from each group were highlighted.

The focus group summaries were synthesized into a final report for the director of the Research Information Center. Overall, the analysis of focus group discussions

- indicated a wide range of unmet information needs;
- identified that communication and coordination problems present barriers to effective use of information;
- provided insights into the current and possible future role of computer technology as a tool for managing information; and
- suggested a number of possible avenues for cooperative efforts to provide more efficient, more effective, and more timely information management.

In its original strategy, the team had planned to use the focus group findings to guide the development of a written questionnaire to survey staff and selected volunteers. After preliminary work, the team decided to discard the written questionnaire with the recommendation that the Center conduct a more targeted survey at a later date.

Interviewing Senior Staff

After reviewing the focus group report, the Center director and the team leaders realized that the information needs of the upper levels of the organization had not been adequately assessed. In *"Tactics for Corporate Library Success"*, Laurence Prusak and James Matarazzo recommend "learn[ing] the information needs of the senior people in your firm" as the first step in becoming "a true information manager."[4] The team leaders determined it was essential to revise the research plan to include interviews with the executive director and division-level staff, mainly division heads. A consultant was retained to direct this effort, with Center staff team members assisting in interviewing. Interviews were scheduled for one hour and audiotaped with permission of the interviewee.

The goal of the interview process was to examine information needs and resources both organizationally from Association and division perspectives, and functionally from staff and management perspectives. Prior to the interview date, interviewees were sent a memorandum outlining the purpose and topics of the interview and were asked to respond for themselves as well as for the staff in their divisions. The interviews began with a brief background on the team's activities and then moved to questions covering information uses, sources, and needs. The interviewers made a special point of exploring ideas about uses of technology and opportunities for interaction between the Center and the division in information dissemination. (The questions are given in Appendix II.)

Because the focus group analysis had indicated that communication and coordination problems were barriers to effective use of information, interviewees were queried about ideas for future actions to improve information access and to better meet information needs. Many of the ideas mentioned involved electronic access.

Among the ideas for future products and services were

- current journal and news articles on specified topics through alert services;
- a frequently updated database of AARP programs, publications, and press releases;
- products with synthesized information similar to the Association fact sheets;
- information on selected topics with abstracts, book reviews, and other aids to reviewing information effectively; and
- an information service with specific information on state organizations and agencies, current and proposed state legislation, and methods of service provision to the older population.

Interviewees thought that information access by staff and volunteers could be improved by

- exploring ways to provide access to both summary and detailed information, depending on user need;

- investigating ways to help field offices gain access to information as quickly as headquarters staff;
- gathering information on key organizations and people involved with issues of central importance to the Association; and
- determining effective means of delivering this information.

Applying Project Findings

"Users want information quickly, and they want it delivered to them. Increasingly they want it delivered in electronic form."[5] Feedback from both senior staff members and focus group participants indicated that many of them needed improved methods of finding accurate information and receiving it quickly and easily. The Center has implemented several projects to begin to address these needs.

During the period of the Research Information Center Marketing Team's activities, the Center director initiated discussions with the Association's Management Information Systems Operation concerning a collaboration to implement an "AARP encyclopedia." This was conceived as a "one-stop-shopping" service providing electronic access to a variety of databases for staff in their offices. The Center's role in the first phase of this collaboration was to define the contents and functional requirements of the encyclopedia. To implement this project, the Center director established the AARP Encyclopedia Team composed of Research Information Center staff. Input from the focus groups and senior staff interviews helped guide the team in identifying an initial group of Association information sources to be included in the encyclopedia.

Two pilot projects offer additional examples of applying the Marketing Team's findings. A Profiling Team set up customized searches of commercial databases for a test group of staff. Another group of staff, selected from a variety of departments, tested the ABI/INFORM database on CD-ROM. Both projects investigated methods of obtaining current, targeted information quickly and easily.

Thinking About the Process and Results

The activities described in this chapter are the beginning steps of an ongoing strategy to examine the information needs of our customers; design, implement, and evaluate products and services; reach more staff and volunteers at all locations; and become the central source of information within the Association. Center staff, while feeling the excitement of moving into new directions, realize that the strategy is complex and time-consuming and requires careful planning and evaluation. "We cannot simply apply computer technology and save a little time for staff doing a little less of the same old thing."[6]

Overall, the work of the Research Information Center Marketing Team has provided a solid basis for the Center to launch its efforts to better meet Association information needs. The project increased the Center's awareness of the need to keep open the channels of communication with all divisions of the Association, to encourage and maintain ongoing contact between all divisions and locations, and to seek more effective means of information management. Most importantly, through the interdisciplinary approach of this project the Center learned to use new and effective strategies, techniques, and tools that will be useful in expanding and evaluating the Center's outreach efforts and in increasing its visibility.

References

1. Durance, Joan C. "Information Needs, Old Song: New Tune" in Mathews, Anne J., series ed, *Rethinking the Library in the Information Age,* vol. II. Washington, D.C.: U.S. Government Printing Office, 1989, 224.0.

2. Templeton, Jane Farley *Focus Groups: A Guide for Marketing and Advertising Professionals.* Chicago: Probus Publishing 1989.

3. Krueger, Richard A. *Focus Groups: A Practical Guide for Applied Research.* Newbury Park, Calif. A: Sage, 1988.

4. Prusak, Laurence, and James M. Matarazzo. "Tactics for Corporate Library Success" Library Journal, 115(15), September 15, 1990 pp. 45-46.

5. Campbell, Jerry D. "Shaking the Conceptual Foundations of Reference: A Perspective" Reference Services Review, 20(4) Winter 1992 29-31.

6. See note 5.

Appendix

I. Focus Group Questions

1. Warm-up questions
    Thinking back to high school or college days, how did you gather information? What did you do?

2. Types of information used on the job
    Think back over the past two or three weeks to a particular time when you needed information for a project at work. Describe the situation, particularly the types of information you needed (e.g., responding to a reporter asking for the number of retirees, preparing a panel presentation that gives an overview of current medical ethics issues, providing background information on property tax relief measures for use by a state legislative committee).
    What types of information have the greatest impact on your job? Do you have a special need for items such as regular updates on a particular topic, summaries of recent research on certain subjects, information about rograms in a particular area of the country?
    What is the most useful information you receive on a regular basis? What source? Why is it important? If you could recommend one improvement in the content or format of this information, what would it be?

3. Methods of obtaining information
    What sources and methods do you use frequently to get the information you need for your job? Do you use office electronic files, journals and other resources kept in your office, contacts with colleagues, staff you assign to gather information?
    What would assist you most in getting information easily and effectively? How do you like your information delivered to you?

4. Use of the Research Information Center (RIC)
    How do you use the RIC, if you do? Do you refer outside calls, request information via the computer, get articles noted in Quick View, request materials from other libraries?
    What keeps you from using the RIC very often or not at all? Do you find information not available quickly enough, no time to go there, RIC staff not familiar enough with topic areas of your job, the online catalog confusing? What one improvement in RIC services would be most helpful to you in your job?

Appendix II. Senior Staff Interview Questions

The Research Information Center Marketing Team has been examining the information needs and resources of AARP staff and volunteers. Through the use of focus groups both at headquarters and in the field, staff and volunteers have provided important insights concerning their information needs. The team is now interviewing senior staff regarding their information needs and the role of the Research Information Center in providing information to the Association.

We have a short list of questions to guide the discussion but welcome any thoughts you have on this topic area. The questions in this interview focus on external types of information rather than internal AARP-generated information, such as personnel or budget data. I think this focus will be apparent through the wording of the questions. We would like to record this session if that's all right with you.

Any questions or comments before we begin the questions?

1. To begin, what are your most valuable sources of information? Probe: meaning of timeliness, efficient means to obtain, preferred format.

2. In your division, what kinds of information do staff and volunteers need and in what ways do they get it?

3. How do you and your staff and volunteers use technology in gathering and disseminating information?

4. In your view, what is the largest unmet information need or information gap within AARP? (This might relate to technology, staff, or communication with volunteers or members, for example.)

5. What role should the Research Information Center play in providing information to your division? How does that role fit with your division's strategic planning?

6. Where do you see an opportunity for greater interaction between the Center and your division in disseminating information to staff, volunteers, and members?

7. As decentralization plays out within your division, how do you think your information needs will change?

8. How would you envision an ideal information system functioning within the Association?

Any other comments? We appreciate your comments and the time you've given to this interview.

Chapter 4
"LV" = Leadership Victory
Kaycee Hale

"ANYONE—at any age and in any circumstance—can become a *leader*.
Becoming a leader is the ultimate act of *free* will."
—Warren Bennis, *On Becoming a Leader*

History and experience teach us that leadership is an essential ingredient for the success of all human activity. A leaderless team is a group of individuals with different agendas without common or unified outcomes. The function of the leader is to establish a vision, articulate shared values, and maintain a high level of verve. Another vital leadership task is the motivation of one's followers... by persuasion, inspiration, role-modeling, integrity, other-esteem, etc.

Michael Maccoby, in his book *Why Work...Motivating and Leading the New Generation,* discusses the concept of the self-developer. He indicates that self-developer leaders have much to offer any organization. They focus on the exceptional management of tangible and intangible resources, upgrading their marketable skills, motivating others, integrating usable information, solving problems, facilitating effective teams, understanding customer needs, and self-esteem. They strive to be competent business visionaries, not compliant bureaucrats. They integrate a substantive inventory of values into their work environment. They mesmerize others with their passionate verve.

Leadership, the position and the person that live by the axiom "good is the enemy of best and best is the enemy of better."

The 1992-93 *Books in Print* lists 400 books under the subject heading Leadership, 147 under Value, and fewer than 10 under both Value and Verve as business subheadings. If we assume that each book contains an average of 250 pages, the conclusion would be that more than 135,000 pages are in print about these four topics. An estimated twenty new books are written each year solely on leadership...up from the annual publication of six books only ten years ago. Based on an average 300 words per page, we could then assume that more than 1.5 million words were written this year alone informing us, teaching us, enlightening and guiding us step by step to the pinnacle of the leadership ladder. If indeed there is such a plethora of information, why is our nation subsumed by the notion that there is a "*void* in the ranks of America's leadership"—*regardless* of the profession?

Does the answer lie in the possibility that fewer leaders are being born today? That is, if we are to infer that leaders are born *instead* of made. Does the answer lie in the lack of individual personal and professional courage to be scrutinized by the public at large? Does the answer lie in the lack of leadership education and training? Could *the* answer be as simple as "train and educate college students to become leaders"? Could the solution be that the Jepson School of Leadership Studies at the University of Richmond (Virginia) has finally stumbled upon an ingenious discovery?

Believed to be the first college of its kind in the United States, the Jepson School (funded by a $20 million gift from businessman alumnus Robert Jepson) offers bachelor degrees in leadership studies. At least forty other American colleges offer leadership courses and/or training. Additionally, corporate, professional association, national, and international workshops, seminars, and academies abound on the topic of leadership.

Can anything be said here that has *not* already been said? Can *any* theory be proposed that has not already been discussed? Can *any* "magic bullet" be propelled that will alter just one person's thinking, or more importantly, change one person's action plan?

As someone ensconced in the apparel industry, I would be remiss for not threading those conceptual fashion fibers into the fabric of Leadership as a *heart* issue, rather than one merely for the head. Leadership carries with it a continuum of risk, the necessity of vision and value, as well as the image of passion, prestige, and status. In such a fickle industry as fashion, anything that was once the purview of the privileged but has now gained wide acceptance ... anything that is in demand by status seekers worldwide for more than a century ... *anything* that is copied, forged, stolen, used as barter, and coveted by most ... *anything* like that deserves a closer inspection. Something like that is perceived as a leader in its own field.

As one of the most highly visible personal and professional status accouterments, such an apparel "thing" is represented by two letters: "LV" (Louis Vuitton). Those "LV" initials on such items as purses, luggage, jewelry, equestrian equipment, apparel, and accessories will now come to mean more than just a leather-goods conglomerate with global distribution and status seekers displaying them worldwide.

For the fashion industry, LV's ubiquitous initials symbolize the essence of this chapter: "LV" = Leadership, which in turn = Vision, Value, and Verve. This type of leadership means that it is (1) there for the taking by anyone, (2) there for anyone willing to commit to a future endeavor, and (3) there for the attainment of one's most passionate goal(s).

Leadership is Multifold and Magic

According to Andrew DuBrin, a human relations expert, "over 10,000 studies have been conducted on the characteristics that contribute to the effectiveness of a leader."[1] Warren Bennis, one of the most published researchers and theorists on the issue of leadership, has noted that there are more than 350 definitions of leadership and thousands of empirical investigations.

Leadership theories proliferate and are as numerous as the theorists and reactive and proactive visionaries who write about them. This chapter could explore such theories as the one that indicates leadership is 15 percent role or positional power, 35 percent expertise power, and 50 percent personality power. Or it could critique such business references as *Leadership and the Quest for Integrity* by Joseph L. Badaracco, Jr. and Richard R. Ellsworth, *Creating Excellence: Managing Corporate Culture, Strategy and Change in the New Age* by Craig R. Hickman and Michael A. Silva, and *Why Work ... Motivating and Leading the New Generation* by Michael Maccoby.

Or it could review more contemporary theories geared to making leaders of us all in fifty minutes or less through the exploration of Crisp Publication titles such as *Leadership Skills for Women* by Marilyn Manning with Patricia Haddock and *Learning to Lead* by Pat Heim and Elwood N. Chapman—both of which are self-study guides less than a hundred pages in length. But the most important nugget you could glean from any source is to remember that *you* do not have to be an executive or a manager to be a leader within a company. Successful companies usually have leaders at every level.

Definitively there are many leadership models—inclusionary, visionary, transformational, transactional, charismatic, situation, autocratic, participatory, democratic, hierarchical, inductive, etc. But which one is best? We must first recognize the fact that there is no single path to leadership, no single definition. There is no distinctive, comprehensive list of leadership qualities. Leadership is not a single trait, nor is it made up of a single predisposition to a particular attitude or to a specific activity.

Lists of leadership skills are available from various theorists in hundreds of journal articles. Just in case you missed some of those articles, the skills lists include—but are not limited to—risk taking, promoting an idea or service or product, influencing others, persuading, motivating groups, inspiring others, initiating, self-directing, persisting, confronting problem situations, active problem solving, planning and promoting change, mediating, reconciling conflicts, negotiating, bargaining, debating, selling, managing time, chairing meetings, making hard decisions, and leading others. So how do we get "there" from "here"? How do we differentiate between our department or organizational management role and our leadership potential? What do we need to know in order to make that quantum leap from manager to leader?

Research studies have shown that leaders are concerned with ideas and vision; managers are concerned with tasks and people. Leaders achieve commitment via inspiration; managers achieve it by involvement. Leaders find problems; managers fix them. Leaders plan long range; managers, short range. Leaders cultivate and are involved in relationships that are intuitive, empathic, and turbulent; managers delineate relations along the steady path that follows the formal, organizational chain of command.[2]

Leadership is *bold*. It is underscored by *courage*—the courage of one's convictions. It values the daring act of risk taking. It torpedoes through the "good enough" barrier. It sees no bounds in the ability to move forward, to provide effectiveness while navigating the information superhighway, well outside structural library walls.

Leadership is about the transformation from "what is" to "what can be." It is about the business that is attentive to progress, rather than mere process. It is the exertion of influence over others to achieve specific objectives in pursuit of excellence. It is about that handful of profound moments in life, at least several of which are centered on someone we greatly admire and respect.

Superior leadership always makes you stand out and above the crowd. Leadership is not about being a library chameleon; it is about becoming a staunch visionary. Leadership is about the messenger as well as the message. It is about serving as a symbol. Leaders leave behind assets and a legacy. Leadership is passionate. It is a heart issue, rather than a head issue. It underscores the fact that "the heart and soul (of an individual) are far greater *energizers* than the mind and logic. The measure of leadership is not the quality of the head, but the tone of the body."[3]

LV = Leadership Vision

Vision: panoramic view, imagination, creation, dream. Dream the vision. Envision the dream, for indeed it is clear vision that creates the future.

Vision is the fuel, the propellant of leadership. Working within the key parameters of organizational goals, department structure, and today's human, tangible, and intangible resources is not nearly enough in this world of nanosecond expectations. Leadership vision is essential. Vision is the camera lens you choose to focus on your future. Your choice can be a close-up portrait, a regular view, or the panoramic vista. Vision is the perceptive image of where the organization is headed. It is the projection of ideas and images that excite people and therefore inspire staff members to do better than their best.

Vision represents "what" to achieve. Leaders must communicate a compelling vision—one that people want to "Make" happen. Jay A. Conger, author of *The Charismatic Leader* calls visionary leaders "meaning makers" because of their ability to give an organization a sense of purpose, a picture of the panoramic view.

Not all visions are created equal. Some are sweeping, broad-brush-stroke silhouettes of the future; some are outlines of a particular new project. Whatever the scope, leaders must infuse their mental state of being with a heavy dose of outcomes. That vision must monopolize their internal mind-set. Leaders develop a one-track, right-brained attitude of accomplishment, augmented by a left-brained bravado of vision. The discriminating approach to leadership results in the most futuristic visions. The analytic avenue channels visions onto the high road of mission statements—those declarations that guide the actions of individuals and organizations.

Individuals in leadership positions think long term—beyond today's crises, beyond the upcoming quarterly report, beyond the horizon, and then some. They look farther than the unit they are directing. They grasp that unit's or department's relationship in a more corporate or global context. They reach and influence constituents removed from their immediate jurisdictions. They venture outside their boundaries with vision and verve; they seek to add value to each encounter they (and their departments) have. They put notable emphasis on the objective and subjective attitudes of vision, values, verve, and motivation. Leaders understand the nonrational and unconscious elements in every leader-constituent interaction. They master the political skill to cope with the conflicting requirements and expectations of varied and sometimes contrasting constituencies. Leaders project their vision with goal setting determination. Their particular style of goal setting permits them to understand the difficulty others have in practicing this skill. Leaders understand and take into account the fact that others do not set goals because they don't want to take responsibility for just how good they can become. Leaders not only anticipate "just how good *they* can become," they stake their intellectual, emotional, and psychological currency on it. They propel their vision to the future with pinpoint accuracy.

In order to maintain the momentum of the vision, Kathleen Lawler-Demitros, vice president of marketing at Harley-Davidson, suggests the following: "Keep a notebook or tape recorder with you all the time. Imagine having conversations about your vision with various key people, and keep track of your best lines, the sharpest selling points, the critical needs it will fulfill. Then organize your ideas into several formats: a sketch, an annotated outline, a proposal, a 25-word summary, a dummy ad or commercial storyboard, a slogan, a mission statement."[4]

The Vision Challenge

Only he who can see the invisible can do the impossible. The future belongs to those who would question the present. Leaders must have a powerful and potent vision in order to turn it into reality.

- *Manage the dream, not the job.* Micromanagement or the "mother-may-I syndrome" reeks of insecurity and shortsightedness. Leaders tend to be action-oriented individuals 75-plus percent of the time. They characteristically are always busy; they are highly competitive; they are quick thinkers; and most assuredly, they must be risk-takers. They produce decisions and solutions; however, they tend to listen only partially to input. They are committed to "getting the job done and getting it done now." They measure results by discovery, breakthrough, and accomplishments. In order to manage the dream, leaders need to understand and to embrace people-oriented, process-oriented, and idea-oriented staff members. Leaders must understand that their use of action-orientation can be construed by their staff as authority rather than persuasion, which is the essence of leadership.

- *Be expansive in your dreams.* Martin Luther King Jr. said, "The ultimate measure of a man [leader] is not where he stands in moments of comfort and convenience, but where he stands at times of challenge, controversy and change." Most of us have worked within an environment where the industry, professional, business, political, and organizational cultural values have been set by white males. The vision of the dominant culture has not overtly focused on how organizational and consumer cultural diversity may impact one's visionary success. Today's leader must take into account the proliferation of changes such as the ones delineated by statistics and other projections by the U. S. Department of Labor, according to Dr. George Simons in *Working Together: How to Become More Effective in a Multicultural Organization.*

> —White males are now less than half of the American work force.
> —By 2025, only 15 percent of those entering the American work force will be white males, 42 percent will be white females and the balance will be African-Americans and immigrants. Nearly one-third of the new entrants will be women and men of color.
> —Immigrants will represent the largest share of the increase of the U. S. population and work force.

Vision ... that panoramic view. Vision ... that multicolored mosaic. Vision ... that which values each organizational member.

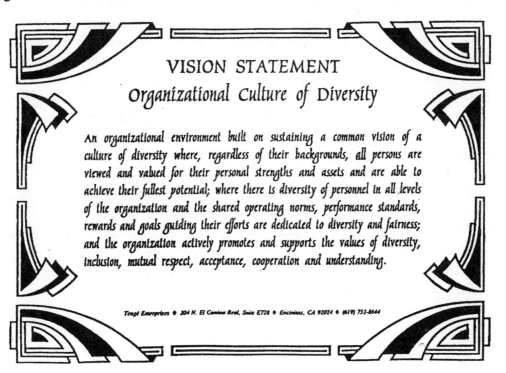

VISION STATEMENT
Organizational Culture of Diversity

An organizational environment built on sustaining a common vision of a culture of diversity where, regardless of their backgrounds, all persons are viewed and valued for their personal strengths and assets and are able to achieve their fullest potential; where there is diversity of personnel in all levels of the organization and the shared operating norms, performance standards, rewards and goals guiding their efforts are dedicated to diversity and fairness; and the organization actively promotes and supports the values of diversity, inclusion, mutual respect, acceptance, cooperation and understanding.

Teagé Enterprises ♦ 204 N. El Camino Real, Suite E728 ♦ Encinitas, CA 92024 ♦ (619) 753-8644

- *Beware of the dangers of myopia.* Curiosity and daring are primary aspects of leadership vision. Peter Drucker said, "No one wants to hear about your labor pains; all they want to see is the baby." Whatever hits the fan will not be equally distributed. Shortsightedness is something you need to eradicate—both yours and that of others. Change can be and frequently is frightening for everyone. Even if things are bad, and even if any progressive change could make them better, everyone seems to still worry about "what if". Staff members often think about, but do not always articulate...What if the change makes things worse instead of better? What if I can't deal well with the change? What if everyone likes the change except me?
These are some of the questions that your Vision will spawn in the minds of others. Myopia focuses on your vision, your agenda of intentions, without taking into account the answers to the questions of others. Without serious consideration of these answers, your vision will be formidably undermined.

- *Look, search, seek out opportunities at all levels of your corporation.* Know that leadership opportunities are not held within the private sanctums of the administrator's office or the executive suite. Seize opportunities: do not wait for them. He who fears to step except where he sees other men's footprints will never make any dynamic, new discoveries.

- *Challenge the status quo.* Look for new "controversial approaches" to long-standing problems. Even if you are on the right track, you are bound to get run over if you just sit there contemplating your navel. Remember that the "difficult is that which can be done immediately; the impossible is that which takes a bit longer" (author unknown).

- Practice relentless IMAGE BUILDING. Enhance the images of yourself, your staff, your organization, and your profession. Marketing one's self and one's library is an ongoing process that requires constant attention. A leader's vision must be enunciated on an ongoing basis, not only to his or her external clientele, but also to one's internal customers.

Marketing...the missile that launches your mission! Marketing...the plan to inform your customers about your product and/or service. Marketing...the publicity, the promotion, and the public relations of your vision. The leader must (1) "define the objectives...what you want to happen with a specific time frame for achieving them, (2) identify your target groups—all possible circles you might have the potential to assist, (3) determine the strategy and tactics for reaching that target market, (4) decide which communication tools to use, and (5) evaluate your success" — according to a *Marketing Still Matters* fact sheet prepared by the Libraries and Community Development Branch, Alberta (Canada) Culture and Multiculturalism Department.

- *Establish a vision framework*. That framework encompasses shared vision, shared norms, shared expectations, shared purposes, shared beliefs, and shared commitment. As a leader, you not only must clearly articulate the vision, norms, expectations, purposes, etc., you also must work deliberately as their champion. You must resolve to be both coach and cheerleader.

- *DARE to dream great dreams!* Leaders do not pray for powers that are equal to their tasks; they pray for tasks that are equal to their powers. Alan Kay said, "The best way to predict the future is to invent it." The high point of your life cannot occur if you keep repeating yesterday. Leaders envision tomorrow and beyond.

LV + Value

Value: importance, benefit, significance, eminence, influence, prestige, power—of the leadership model.

Value characterizes the "how" of the vision, those pivotal beliefs about what it will take to succeed and how people will interact in order to carry out the vision. The "how," of course, is based on decision-making techniques resulting from judgment calls dictated by complex variables. Decision-making—sound judgment practices—is the essence of the primary risk-taking adventures of leadership. Peter Drucker notes that in a narrow sense every decision is a judgment. Each decision is "a choice between alternatives. It is rarely a choice between right and wrong. It is at best a choice between 'almost right' and 'almost wrong'—but much more often a choice between two courses of action, neither of which is probably more nearly right than the other." [5]

The core value of "being the best" is often the most sought-after vision. "Being the best" is transitory; it is highly illusive. I would define it, not as the quality of the product, but rather as the satisfaction provided to the customer, based on the customer's expectation. Quality was once yesterday's extra, but is today's expectation and will be tomorrow's essential. If we try to make it purely a prescriptive, an off-the-shelf, one-size-fits-all approach to customer service ... if we do not apply more vision and verve to this prescription, TQM (total quality mangement) will soon join the ranks of the once "hot topic" MBO (management by objectives). Leaders understand that "customer satisfaction" is not their reliance on library standard practices and procedures, but rather on the clients' perception of any delivery of library services to their preconceived satisfaction.

Inasmuch as there is a common perception that "managers are occupied with doing things right, leaders are those who pre-occupied with doing the right things," states Burt Nanus, author of *Doing the Right Thing*. Further, he writes profusely on the predominance of managers and the absence of leaders in most organizations.

Value is inconclusive of intellectual and creative currency, as well as human and materials asset capital. Value includes the caliber of our products—tangible and intangible—in both the organizational and the external environment.

The Value Capital

Values do not thrive very well when psychosclerosis and homeostasis are present within the work environment. Psychosclerosis is the "hardening of one's attitudes"; homeostasis is defined as "maintaining the status quo." Increase your (and your department's) value as follows.

- *Verbalize and affirm the value of the vision.* Someone is doing the same thing over and over again and expecting different results. The "how" of vision implementation requires tremendous flexibility. Flexibility is strength. Think bamboo, not oak.
- *Understand and embrace the premise that change is the norm.* Flexibility is the key to complexity and ambiguity. Leaders change their minds quickly, trust their own hunches over other people's facts, and encourage their staffs to ignore habits and experience.

- *Subsume error-making as a component of invaluable new and innovative ideas.* Obstacles are those frightful things you see when you take your eyes off the value of your vision. Leaders must not be afraid to make mistakes and must admit them when they do. They must create an atmosphere in which risk taking is encouraged. They must also be tolerant with those who make mistakes. Difficult it is; impossible it is not!

- *Be driven to exploit new technology.* The tools of the information dissemination occupation must not become the reason for the profession. Information leaders must remain cognizant that they may all be drowning in data and information, but their customers are starving for intelligence, knowledge and analysis. John Naisbitt uses the formula "high tech/high touch" to describe the way human beings should respond to technology. His theory is that whenever something new and glitzy happens in technology (high tech), there must be a counterbalancing human response (high touch). Leaders must remember that the more technology there is in any society, the more people want to be with people. Leadership is a "people" role.

   Leaders must strive to incorporate the tools of technology into their vision, without permitting technology to become the be-all, end-all. Vision should be conceived alongside the value that technology has to offer in order to render efficiency for our customers and effectiveness for our staffs.

- *Generate a constant flow of new ideas valuable to the problem solving process.* Originality in problem solving is frequently the first step in moving beyond what seems impossible. Problem solving is perhaps the greatest communal risk-taking venture of the group process. One common problem solving technique utilizes the following seven steps: Identify the issue of concern; set the outcome goals; analyze the problem; generate potential possibilities; select and plan a solution; implement the decision; and evaluate the outcome.

- *Foster collaboration in getting others to contribute fully to the values process.* Such collaboration must also be imbued with the essence of people (with varying agendas) working together. Leaders could take a lesson from the sports pages here. A successful leader gives the right job to the right person at the right time. Goals are achieved by utilizing all the talents of all team members—regardless of their occupational titles. Leaders build team spirit by knowing how to strategize success for each group member by generating total team achievement.

   Leaders must know that the organizational chart is rarely the best model for positive group dynamics. They must know (1) how to organize the group, (2) which policies and procedures used to manage the work of the group will support both task and maintenance needs, (3) how to elicit the strongest interpersonal relationships so that each group member can effectively interact with every other group member, and (4) how to develop appropriate intergroup relationships.

- *Increase your exposure to, education of, and experiences with other cultures.* Leaders are keenly aware that the future will bring more multiculturalism and multinationalsim, not less. Both national and international leaders face the challenge of uniting different individuals and groups with a focus toward a common values system. "Cultural diversity" is indeed one of this decade's management and leadership buzzword phrases. Leaders cannot remain securely entrenched in their own and their identifiable group's comfort zone. Cross-cultural situations are occurring with greater frequency in the workplace among workers, as well as between library staff members and customers.

NO QUICK FIX! -- Stages Towards a "Culture of Diversity"

CULTURE OF DIVERSITY
An empowering environment,
beyond "managing diversity,"
where all employees are
viewed and valued for their
personal assets and strengths,
and are able to achieve their
fullest potential.

SYSTEMS ALIGNMENT
Policies and procedures,
evaluations, rewards and
promotions, coaching and
counseling, training and
orientation all reflect an
organizational/management
commitment to diversity.

TRANSITIONAL STAGE
Core support groups form, a
task force is normally in
place, awareness training is
implemented, and the
organization installs initiatives
to move into its next stage.

DEVELOPMENTAL STAGE
Organization explores corporate
culture to determine roadblocks
to progress. Mentorship or
coaching programs are discussed
and management skills training
is implemented along with
targeted group training.

*These
are the
passages/
stages an
organization
experiences
as it climbs
toward reaching a
culture of diversity.
To be effective, the
stages must be
"transformational" —
change must be
experienced individually
and culturally within the
organization and have a
positive effect on the mission,
purpose, commitment,
understanding, business
judgement and behavior of
all employees.
Stages are not always
concurrent and occasionally
an organization can be in two
stages at the same time. It is
also true that different departments
and divisions within an organization
can be in different stages.*

AWARENESS STAGE
Usually triggered by a realization
that a "glass ceiling" is in place
because targeted group members
are skewed at the bottom of the
pyramid or are absent, a high
turnover, and few candidates
"in the pipeline."

° Adapted from New Beginnings Management Consulting and Training Services (1992).

Leaders must educate themselves (or seek professional training) in order to understand the differences in such common workplace communication factors as verbal language, humor, gestures, space, time, and touch.

George Simons, author of *Working Together: How to Become More Effective in a Multicultural Organization*, said, "If we take into allowance (1) the individual, (2) his/her personality, (3) his or her cultural background, and (4) the situation, then we start to reach the whole person [the follower who must pursue the Value of the leader's vision]." This statement indicates that there is no such thing as a quick fix. In order to successfully realize his vision, the leader (within the organizational framework) must lead his followers through specific stages to achieve a culture of valued and valuable individuals.

- *Be willing to encourage dissent*. Leaders need people around them who have contrary views, who will play the devil's advocates. Some of the values here require more attention to the task orientation of the followers than to the process structured by the group or the vision outlined by the leader. Task-oriented behaviors essential to a leader include initiating (making suggestions or proposing new ideas), information gathering (asking questions for clarification), opinion seeking (asking for viewpoints about the values or the relative merits of member ideas), brainstorming, but most importantly listening.

- *Realize that intrinsic rewards such as achievement, personal growth, challenge, satisfaction, and quality of work life are frequently more valuable to team members than extrinsic rewards.* Empowerment, as well as encouragement, belongs in the arsenal of leadership skills. Empowerment is the process by which the employee nearest to a service problem is automatically authorized to decide what needs to be done and then does it. The employee, therefore, feels valued in the achievement of the leader's vision. When that privilege is afforded all group members, this permits the leader of the group to use his or her time much more effectively. Empowerment is the process of releasing the expression of personal power to be able to perform the service for which libraries are supposed to be known. Empowerment incorporates shared-decision-making and participative-management practices while implementing systems that help individuals take responsibility for their own work and career development.

  Encouragement is the process of catching people doing things right. It incorporates leadership sensitivity with output-orientation. It enhances group morale—highly valuable organizational ambiance. It underscores Frederick J. Herzberg's motivational theory of security, belonging, recognition, quality of work, and self-actualization. People are motivated when they can look up to someone who does not look down on them.

- *Incorporate the concept that a reorganization of one's department to be more adaptive to customer satisfaction is a valuable marketing strategy.* Leaders must become their own customers with scheduled frequency. They must test and scrutinize their systems from the customer's vantage point. Leaders must subscribe to the theory that indeed it is the customer who defines quality. Leaders understand that quality is a "journey—not a destination." They endorse "relationship marketing" or the development of long-term bonds with customers by making customers feel good about how the library does business and how the library gives them some kind of personal connection to the organizational entity.

- *Possess and publicly exhibit tenacity.* It is up to the leader to convey a positive outlook and to articulate a specific direction toward a favorable future even when business and/or organizational conditions are at their worst. Leaders are four-wheel driven to "no excuses, just results." Leaders are masters of R&R—realism and resilience. Realism provides them with the pragmatism to assess their environment accurately—economically, socially, and politically. Resilience amounts to their ability to bounce back with knee-jerk accuracy. They combine both realism and resilience with a "do-it" mentality.

- *Practice modeling the innovative techniques of others.* Read copiously. Listen and observe. Beg, borrow, and steal ideas from others—not just in special libraries, but also in the public and private sector information centers.
- *Make your customer go "wow."* Happy customers tell eight others; unhappy ones forewarn sixteen. Quantitatively and qualitatively, which information transfer ensures that the value of your risk taking will be rewarded?

Motivated people have aims and values. They are driven by something most of us consider instinctual: survival relatedness, information, mastery, dignity, and meaning. Value exudes risk-taking based on creativity and dedication. To gain more, you have to risk more!

LV = Leadership Verve

Verve: energy, activity, dynamism, enthusiasm, spirit, force, inspiration, the passion for the project.

Leaders are those unique individuals who remain focused on their vision, who center themselves on essential values, and who utilize verve in today's environment of competitive buyouts, rightsizing sell-offs, and lean and mean restructuring of global corporations.

The Verve Charge

Verve is the result of people motivated when they are convinced that they are doing something exceptional. Vision is the substance; verve is the style.

- *Model what you want in terms of energy, action-orientation, and self-confidence.* Leadership is a physically, mentally, and emotionally demanding inner quest resulting in predetermined results. Role-modeling is the process which enhances that outgrowth of self-development. You have to "stand *up*" and "stand *for*" something in order to capture the imagination of others. Effective leaders are self-confident individuals who operate from an internal belief—the belief that one is the primary cause of events happening to oneself, rather than an external (outside forces) locus of control. Leaders are driven by an insatiable need for *self*-fulfillment. They are fully aware that self-concept is destiny.
- *Communicate the proficiency of commitment.* Modern technology has brought increasingly faster modes of communication. Leaders must understand that communication is far more than the spoken (or written) word; it is the power of persuasion. Albert Mehrabian states that 55 percent of any face-to-face message is nonverbal; voice is 38 percent; and words are a mere 7percent. Such nonverbal factors as posture, movement, touch, space, eye contact, facial expression, and appearance are an indication of commitment to your vision. Effective communication is considered so vital in leadership that it is often called "the glue that holds the organization together." It is said that you cannot not communicate. Leaders make certain that they communicate their message in all forums with equal ease.

- *Enhance your charisma quotient.* What is "charisma" anyway? Everyone knows it when they see it, but very few people can tell you exactly what it is. Charisma equals personality, self-confidence, assertiveness, ambition, optimism and a sense of humor. Humor is the closest distance between two people, a universal language, a prescription for stress, the organizational booster of performance, productivity and creativity, the antidote to workplace boredom. Try reading *Anatomy of an Illness* by Norman Cousins if you don't believe in its unorthodox leadership attributes of humor.

- *Develop your political skills.* Strive for social boldness. Be crafty enough to know how to play the political games, negotiate fiscal resources, and gain essential concessions. Corporate politics are a reality—right or wrong, good or bad. Knowing how to play the game and knowing the key players in each game are as vital to your leadership role as knowing which game is being played. Leaders are astute students of the corporate culture and are keenly aware of the prioritized values of the organization in which they reside. In the leadership role, knowing your job is expected. Knowing the political landscape is critical.

- *Take charge. Make your actions speak for you.* Create and sustain a forward, self-directed momentum. Leaders appear to be the writer, director, producer, and headliner of their own Broadway theatrical creation. They are never seen as a bit player in someone else's production. Leaders uphold a positive self-expectancy, a positive self-image, positive self-control, positive self-esteem, positive self-awareness, positive self-motivation, positive self-discipline, and positive self-projection.

- *Get out in front.* Representing your group in its dealings with others is a substantial leadership task. A distinctive characteristic of the most competent leaders is that they do not shrink from external representation. They see the long-term needs and goals of their constituency in the broadest context, and they act accordingly. They know the value of public speaking and they do it with frequency. Leaders endorse the speaker "Be-Attitudes." Be alive, be informative. Be likable, flexible, creative, committed. Be *memorable*!

- *Develop stamina.* Always remain active. Stay on your feet; move about. Learn how to conserve energy and store it up for critical times. The ethics of rational self-interest dictate that care must be taken to preserve the physical, emotional, and psychological anatomy of the leader. Rational selfishness mandates that every leader develop techniques for stress release and relaxation. Stamina is attained when a rational balance is achieved between work and play and between personal and professional goals. A healthy mind and body are interdependent, and a positive mental attitude is probably the single most important component.

- *Become a spiritual leader—preaching for causes, upholding ideals, and using symbols to motivate and inspire others.* Leaders know that if they can change behaviors, they can change attitudes, eventually getting others to think differently and adopt new values. Leaders must identify what motivates and inspires their followers—self-preservation, money, power, position, fulfillment, affiliation, fame, etc. They need to know how to generate that "feel good" ambiance.

- *Exude passion.* Inside the organization, become known as the leader who is compelling, the one who sways others by reasoning to a higher than cerebral power. Develop public speaking skills to mesmerize listeners because they so rarely hear. Tap into people's emotions through a disciplined display of one's own passion and use passion as the valuable tool it is in selling one's vision.

- *Radiate enthusiasm.* If you don't have enthusiasm that is contagious, whatever you do have is also contagious.

In Praise of Followship

Vision, value, and verve do not a leader make. Leaders must have followers in order to complete their visionary objectives. A leader's effectiveness is judged by his or her followers' performance. In order to earn such a degree of trust and loyalty, a leader must exemplify an integration of ethical values.

Leadership implies integrity—a wholeness, a unity of oneness. Personal integrity also suggests a firm adherence to a system of ethics, a hierarchy of core belief that are progressively formulated by each individual and tested repeatedly in the matrix of one's personal and professional lives. The completeness of integrity demands an integrated compatibility of values. This insinuates an inner moral compass, a reliability, a conscience. Thus leadership rests on a firm foundation of the individual's own capabilities, drive, and ethical behavior.

Leaders who succeed in the last decade of this century will be the organization and people builders. They will foresee the strategic talent mandates required to nourish the critical fitness of their visionary future. They will invest in building corporate and personal capabilities essential to the short-term survival and long-term success of the institutional or departmental entity.

Each step of the leadership path is forged with a plan to develop future successors. They will create a high caliber of group efficiency as well as team effectiveness. They develop their followers by inspiring them to do more than they thought they could. The goal of the common leader is to get the people to think highly of the leader; the goal of the *exceptional* leader is to get the people to think highly of themselves.

The essence of leadership is balanced by the essential component of followship. Leaders frequently have their privilege, but some forget that followers have their rights:

The Followship
Bill of Rights

1. Each follower has the right to work in a climate in which self-initiative and pride can flourish.
2. Each follower has the right to communicate up the chain of command and to have his or her ideas considered.
3. Each follower has the right to work in a morale-building environment.
4. Each follower has the right to be involved in doing something exceptional.
5. Each follower has the right to be included in collective recognition—points of personal identification that people can readily share.
6. Each follower has the right to have his or her strengths utilized and to achieve self-fulfillment.
7. Each follower has the right to be stretched to his or her fullest potential and to become a hero.
8. Each follower has the right to be a problem-solver.
9. Each follower has the right to be coached, to be taught how to win, and to share in the victory celebration and accolades.
10. Each follower has the right to be inspired by trust, courage, integrity, accountability, and passion.

11. Each follower has the right to feel esteemed—valuable to the group as a person.
12. Each follower has the right to information regarding more than just policies and procedures.
13. Each follower has the right to know what the vision expectations are, to know how to meet them, and to receive feedback regarding how the expectations have or have not been met.

LV

"LV." Leadership. Vision. Value. Verve. Leadership has got to be in somebody's face, *every*body's face. It is the understanding that the concept of "if we build it, they will come" is for baseball diamonds and dead heroes only. It is about the inestimable grace of the messenger and the invaluable gravity of the message. It is the clear shot between your heart and your head—the bonding of ideas, ideals, and execution.

Leadership: the ergonomics of today's workplace! It is the essential fit that results from multi faceted factors being taken into consideration based on the progressive productivity of satisfying the customer and the task orientation of staff members whose strengths are consistently utilized.

Bibliography

Books

Badaracco, Joseph L., Jr. and Richard R. Ellsworth. *Leadership and the Quest for Integrity.* Boston: Harvard Business School Press, 1988.

Bennis, Warren. *On Becoming a Leader.* Reading, Mass.: Addison-Wesley, 1989.

Cohen, William A. *The Art of the Leader.* New York: Prentice-Hall, 1989.

Conger, Jay A. *The Charismatic Leader: Behind the Mystique of Exceptional Leadership.* San Francisco: Jossey-Bass, 1989.

DuBrin, Andrew J. *Human Relations for Career and Personal Success*, 2nd edition. New York: Prentice-Hall, 1988.

Gardenswartz, Lee, and Anita Rowe. *What It Takes.* New York: Doubleday, 1987.

Heim, Pat, and Elwood N. Chapman. *Learning to Lead.* Los Altos, Calif.: Crisp Publications.

Hickman, Craig R., and Michael A. Silva. *Creating Excellence: Managing Corporate Culture, Strategy and Change in the New Age.*

Kouzes, Jim, and Barry Posner. *The Leadership Challenge.* San Francisco: Jossey-Bass, 1987.

Lang, Doe. *The Secret Of Charisma.* New York: New Choices Press, 1982.

Maccoby, Michael. *Why Work ... Motivating and Leading the New Generation.* New York: Simon & Schuster, 1989.

Manning, Marilyn, and Patricia Haddock. *Leadership Skills for Women.* Los Altos, Calif.: Crisp Publications.

McCall, Morgan, Jr., and Robert Kaplan. *Whatever It Takes: Decision Makers at Work.* Englewood Cliffs, N. J., Prentice-Hall, 1985.

Nanus, Burt. *Doing the Right Thing.*

Simons, George. *Working Together: How to Become More Effective in a Multicultural Organization.* Los Altos, Calif.: Crisp Publications, 1989.

W. Warner Burke Associates, Inc. *Leadership Report,* 2nd edition. New York: W. Warner Burke Associates, 1988.

Articles

DePree, Max. "Leadership Is an Art ... Book Summary of the Month." *Success Magazine.* XXXVII (3): 1990 p. 48.

Horton, Thomas, R. "Qualities of a Successful CEO." *Hyatt Magazine,* Fall 1987 pp. 22-27. Title discontinued.

"Needed for the 21st Century: A New Kind of Leadership." *Inside Retailing.* vol VI, (13): Lebhar-Friedman, Inc. p.1. (April 8, 1991).

Stoltenberg, John. "See the Big Picture? Now Show Your Staff," *Working Women, 15.*
        April 1990, (no.4), pp. 84-86, 126.
Zaleznik, A. "Managers and Leaders: Are They Different?" *Harvard Business
        Review, 55* (3), 1977, pp. 55, 67-78.

References

1. Dubrin, Andrew J. *Human Relations for Career and Personal Success.* New York: Prentice-Hall, 2nd edition, 1988, p. 366.
2. W. Warner Burke Associates, Inc. *Leadership Report.* New York: W. Warner Burke Associates, 2nd edition, 1988, pp. 4, 17.
3. DePree, Max. "Leadership Is an Art ... Book Summary of the Month," *Success Magazine*, XXXVII (3), April 1990, p. 48.
4. John Stoltenberg. "See the Big Picture? Now Show Your Staff." *Working Woman* 15 (no. 4). April 1990. P 85.
5. Thomas R. Horton. "Qualities of a Successful CEO." *Hyatt Magazine.* Fall 1987. P 23. Title discontinued.

Chapter 5
Know Your Company and Its Business
Lou B. Parris

Librarianship qualifies as a profession partly because it is based on a "body of knowledge" that has broad application. To make that knowledge work successfully, though, we must apply it in a particular organizational setting or context. Each organization is different, and the successful librarians are the ones who know the character and personality of the organization and are able to work within it, and to align themselves with its vision and culture. Corporate librarians historically have been allied closely with their organizations, but as we adopt the new business paradigms of interdependence and partnering, intimate knowledge of the company and its business is an even more essential requirement for success.

The material in this chapter is an outgrowth of talks presented to the special libraries classes at the University of Texas Graduate School of Library and Information Science. The talks were subtitled "What it took me twenty years to learn," and they were intended to introduce prospective corporate librarians to the corporate workplace and provide them with a sort of game plan for becoming thoroughly acquainted with the companies in which they would work. In this chapter I identify some of the many aspects of "knowing your company" that will contribute to the librarian's success. I am not suggesting that there is a cookbook for becoming an overnight company expert. The process of becoming acculturated happens over time and through experience, but it can be accelerated by having a good idea of what makes a company work and by deliberately setting out to gather knowledge and identify resources that can keep librarians abreast of company activities. This chapter probably will be most useful to librarians new to the corporate environment, but it also may be helpful to those joining a different organization or wanting to gain more knowledge about their present company.

Information Resources

Before we proceed to identify some of the things successful librarians should know about the companies that employ them, let me suggest some key sources of information. Here there is some really good news. Librarians are in an excellent position to access many essential resources. Books, journals, newspapers, and databases are all readily available. The library may also be the repository of company publications such as in-house magazines and newsletters, histories, and other useful documents.

In addition to these publications a number of other resources are readily available.

- *Company manuals.* The company may produce a number of manuals giving guidance and direction to employees about using various company resources. Manuals of a general nature, such as the employee handbook, the company policy manual, or the safety manual, should be read immediately and kept available for convenient reference. Manuals guiding employees in the use of various facilities and services should be collected and used for reference as needed.
- *Computer bulletin boards or in-house news services.* Many companies utilize their computer networks to broadcast daily news and information about company activities or industry news.
- *Supervisors.* Officially, the supervisor is the employee's source of information. Librarians should take every opportunity to obtain their supervisors' insights into the workings of the organization and the personalities of its leaders.
- *Mentors.* If the company does not have a formal mentoring program, identifying one or more individuals who can perform that function can be extremely helpful. One of the best reasons for having a mentor is to have a guide around the organization. It is good to have more than one — one perhaps in the information area (if the organization is large enough) and another from elsewhere in the company. Mentors should be individuals who know the organization well and who are successful in working within it.
- *Professional Colleagues.* If the library has other professional staff, they will be a principal resource for information. Of course, these people must be credible. It is prudent to do some double-checking to verify that you are being given accurate, up-to-date information. If you find that a colleague is frequently giving incorrect or out-of-date information, find another resource!
- *Associates.* Customers and others in the organization with whom you do business can become excellent sources of current information about activities in other parts of the organization. Making it a practice to stay in touch with people from other groups will help you be aware of their special concerns and current developments in their areas that may affect your activities.
- *Orientation and assimilation activities.* Larger organizations usually have some formal orientation activities. These range from a brief session to elaborate processes with mentors and buddy systems that are designed to assimilate employees into the organization.

Understanding the Big Picture

It is essential to be familiar with the industry that the company does business in and the company's place and role in it. All industries are affected by social and political events as well as economic and technical changes. Forces from outside and from within the industry provide both opportunities and threats that will be necessary to understand. Knowing where your industry sits and what to watch for that may affect it will give you the advantage in adjusting to change. You should understand your industry's role in your local environment and economy and its place in society.

Conscientiously reading the main trade journals and newsletters of your industry is essential. Regular database updates from news services will give current information tailored to highlight the topics most relevant to the company's business. If the industry you work in is mature, its history may be recorded in textbooks and the stories of its leaders in biographies.

Part of knowing the industry, of course, is knowing the competition. You should know who your company's chief competitors are and what their relative competitive positions are in the industry. Providing this information to library customers will probably be part of the job anyway.

Knowing the Company's Business

Next, let us focus on the company itself. First, what business is the company in? What are its main products and services? Who are its customers? Central to knowing the company's business is a profound understanding of its vision and mission. If the company has a well-crafted mission statement, it will distinguish that organization from all others. Currently, it is popular to publish and prominently display the company's vision and mission. Many companies reinforce their mission statements with processes that measure company activities against the stated mission. Supervisors or mentors can provide insights into the thinking behind the words of the mission.

Closely associated with a company's vision and mission are statements about its values and beliefs. These statements speak to how the mission is achieved and how employees will be treated and will behave toward each other. Much of the company culture is codified in these statements.

In addition to publications already mentioned, a primary resource for understanding the company's business (for publicly held companies) is the annual report. If, however, the company is very large, the annual report may deal with the corporation as a whole, but not divulge much about individual units. The annual report provides information about financial status, key management, and business activities. Since annual reports are designed to present the company in its best light, some of the challenges the company faces may not be readily apparent. Nonetheless, this is essential reading. Reading reports from earlier years, not just the current year's report, will give some perspective on the company's progress.

What products and/or services does the company deal in? You should develop an understanding of the relative importance of the various products to the company's profitability. If yours is a large organization, you should understand both your organizational unit's products and services and those of other parts of the company. This will be especially true if the library provides service to these other groups, but even if it does not, an understanding of the corporation's business interests is still valuable.

Organizational Structure

This is the formal structure of the company that defines working relationships among its units and people. Successful navigation of the organization requires an understanding of this structure and a map to chart the course. This map, the organization chart, provides a guide to the size and shape of the organization and shows working relationships. It also identifies individuals who hold key positions. It is important to understand why the company is organized as it is, what the various units do, and how they relate to each other. The structure of the chart is also a clue to the culture of the company. The traditional pyramidal shape probably reflects a traditional organization, while a matrix organization or some other form may indicate a different organizational style. A large company will have many levels of organization charts ranging from those that show major company functional units to those indicating the detailed staffing of each unit. Multicompany or multidivision corporations will have charts for each company. A collection of these charts is a valuable tool for library staff. It is worthwhile, also, to look at older organization charts to see how the organization has changed over time.

Once you have a mental picture of the organization chart, the next step is to put faces to the names on it. In a small organization, that will happen easily. In a larger organization, it requires a definite effort. Some companies have "picture books" of the staff. This makes putting faces with the names much easier. If such a resource is not available, you must find other ways to get this information. Supervisors can provide introductions to their superiors, if they have not already done so. Mentors, associates, and colleagues can point out the faces you need to learn and can introduce you to their management. Becoming involved in company activities such as volunteer efforts, recreational events, and cross-functional teams provides excellent opportunities to meet other individuals in the company. Not only will you learn who the people are, but they will learn who you are, thus adding to your visibility as a member of the company team.

Become familiar with the company's site. If you have not been given a copy of the facilities and office plan, obtain one and become familiar with it. Asking your customers for tours of their areas and delivering products instead of mailing them are easy ways to become familiar with areas you do not normally visit.

If the company has other operating units away from the immediate location, you will want to know what these units do and to understand their relationship to your unit. It should become your regular custom to be able to identify any new customer or contact not only by name but by organizational position as well.

It is very important, of course, to be acquainted as closely as possible with the organizational units parallel to yours—the libraries, information centers, etc., in any affiliated organizations. Good working relationships with the other information people in your company will be a key to maximizing benefits and minimizing costs through cooperative ventures and resource and skill sharing. There may be a formal or an informal network of information colleagues throughout the company. Many large companies take advantage of the Special Libraries Association's annual conference to organize company information meetings or social events.

You should take advantage of any opportunities to visit other sites. These visits can be done in connection with business travel as you promote services, work on cooperative ventures, or meet with customers. If personal travel takes you to an area where an affiliated organization is located, it is often possible to arrange for extra time for a visit.

Company Policies

Most companies have stated policies that promote consistency in the company's treatment of employees and establish common standards of employee behavior in how business is conducted. I have mentioned the company policy manual as an valuable information resource. In this section I highlight a few policy areas that are likely to affect librarians.

Most companies have stated policies that promote consistency in the company's treatment of employees who represent the company to the outside world. Most companies have statements regarding ethical conduct in business dealings. It cannot be said too strongly that these statements should be taken very seriously.

There may be specific policies regarding communicating with the press or with the community as a spokesperson for the company. There may also be specific policies regarding how you should communicate with potential employers of previous employees or with potential customers of your vendors. For example, policies may restrict any comments regarding previous employees' performance or any statements that endorse or fail to endorse particular vendors. The company may not allow its name to be used in advertising without management approval. It may have restrictions on gifts or entertainment that employees can receive from vendors.

It is important to know the company's policy and practice regarding participation in outside activities such as civic or professional associations. In some companies, this is a clearly stated policy, but if it is not, you should find out if such participation is highly regarded, merely tolerated, or not favored.

Closely akin to participating in outside activities is the company's policy toward publishing outside the company. This may be encouraged and rewarded or, unlike in the academic community, it may be merely tolerated or actually discouraged. If publication is supported, there may a process for obtaining approval to publish, for having the publication reviewed by the legal department or management, and for handling the assignment of copyright and other rights. Compensation for publication or for speaking engagements may be allowed by the company, or it may not.

Administrative Processes

Every company has a number of administrative processes used to accomplish its business. An understanding of how these processes work, their timing, and their interrelationship is necessary to effective library operation.

- *Planning process.* This is the process that sets the company's overall goals for the year and further sets the plans for each part of the company. Knowing the process for developing these plans, the timing of the planning steps, and the methods used to measure and administer the results of the plans will assist you in managing your own planning process. It will also help you help your customers as they need information resources to develop their plans.

- In addition to the planning process for the current year, there may be longer-term plans (strategic plans, five-year plans, long-range plans). Understanding of the company's longer-term view will give direction to the library's planning process.

- *Budgeting process.* The budgeting process may be closely tied to the planning process, or it may not. This very process determines who gets how much money, and for what. Each company has its particular budget or forecast method and style. Even if you do not have the primary responsibility for preparing a budget, understanding the process will allow you to fit your fiscal needs in at the right time and with the proper justification. Most budgets are divided into capital and expense categories. It is necessary to understand which budget items fall into which class and the differences in how capital and expense items are handled in the process. Probably the hardest thing about the budget process is to become accustomed to thinking more than a year ahead about projected expenses.

- *Approval process for projects.* This process is related to the budget process. This means that projects planned for one year need to be accounted for in the budget that is prepared the year before. Understanding the company's practices regarding cost justification is particularly helpful here. Major projects usually require some kind of cost/benefit analysis. Identifying "hard credits" or actual dollars saved is relatively straightforward. How "soft credits," that is, benefits that cannot be quantified in dollars and cents terms and "funny money" or internal costs, can be used as cost justification is more dependent on the company's practices.

- *Recruiting and employment process.* An understanding of this process will be necessary when adding or replacing staff. Many companies have a preference for filling positions from within when possible. This may work well for filling clerical positions, but unless the organization is very large, this may not be suitable for professional positions. The human resources (or equivalent) department usually has primary responsibility for managing this process, but its decision-making role varies from company to company. You will want to understand the various processes for advertising for candidates, interviewing, and selection. Other aspects of this process are company practices for managing diversity in staffing, internal transfers, and relocation policies.

- *Performance management process.* This is the process that affects all employees, whether or not they are in managerial or supervisory positions. Most companies have some sort of employee evaluation system and base promotions and compensation to some extent on this evaluation. You should understand from the beginning the criteria that will be used to evaluate your performance and who will be evaluating you. Traditionally, the supervisor and her or his supervisors evaluate employees. However, other systems are sometimes used. Self-evaluations, peer evaluations, upward evaluations (subordinates evaluate supervisors), team evaluations, or combinations of these are alternatives to the more traditional forms.

  For librarians in supervisory positions with responsibilities for evaluating staff, this process will be absolutely critical. You should know the criteria used to make the evaluations, the frequency of evaluations, the process used to communicate evaluations to employees, and the process used to follow up on evaluations. Many companies have training sessions to explain these processes, but their timing may not be just right for your needs. In that case, your supervisor and the human resources department can provide guidance.

- *Safety and security.* Most companies have systems or processes that address employee safety and resource security. It is important to understand what your responsibilities are in terms of both. Safety may involve workplace inspections, assuring that all equipment and facilities meet certain standards and that fire and other safety equipment is in place. The library may be responsible for maintaining safety publications. Security processes ensure that company property and facilities are properly protected. Another aspect of security is the protection of proprietary material. You should be thoroughly familiar with any policies or guidelines regarding the handling of company documents. This includes providing access, storing, transporting, or releasing internal documents outside the company.

Service Organizations

- Within every company there is, in addition to the groups that do the main business of the company, various administrative and service groups that facilitate the company's operations. More often than not, the library is one of these service groups. I have identified several others of these below and indicated what dealings the library is likely to have with them. Large organizations will have these and maybe more; smaller organizations will have most. They may be organized differently or have different names, but most companies will have a person or group that provides the service.
- *Human resources.* I have mentioned this group in connection with recruiting and employment processes. It is also typically involved in compensation, performance management, benefits, affirmative action, diversity management, and sometimes training.
- *Law.* This department is involved with contracts, license agreements, patents and other intellectual property rights, regulatory compliance, and litigation. Librarians work with this group, for example, to buy or lease software, contract with consultants and vendors, or manage copyright activities. You should understand the procedure for obtaining legal services and the history of any legal affairs the library has been involved in.
- *Purchasing.* This group handles purchases of materials and services for the company. You should understand the process required to submit purchase requests, the approval process, and the services this group provides in terms of identifying vendors and negotiating best prices. Especially in a large company, this group can provide considerable cost and service advantages by negotiating national contracts and setting up supplier partnerships.
- In some companies, library materials are purchased by this group. In others, the library acts as its own purchasing department for library materials. If the library does its own purchasing, you will want to work with the purchasing group to ensure that the library's procedures comply with company standards and that the library is receiving benefits the purchasing department can offer.
- *Mail, shipping and receiving.* Understanding the operations of this department can make your mailing and shipping operations timely and cost-effective. In large companies, there may be special mailing arrangements within the company, special courier services, service contracts with import and export agents, and other efficiencies that the library can use to advantage.
- *Communications.* The communications group provides internal and external telecommunication services including telephone, voice mail, and sometimes facsimile. Understanding the services provided by this group can help you to be cost-effective in managing your local and long distance communications.
- *Facilities.* This group manages space allocation, construction, office and furniture moves, maintenance, utilities, and sometimes safety and security. Understanding the procedures, scheduling and documentation requirements, and the services available can reduce frustration and assure that your service needs are met.

- *Financial.* This department is responsible for managing the company's financial assets and providing management with data and reports to help them manage their various financial resources. The library will probably deal most regularly with the part of that group that pays vendors for materials and services. You will need a good understanding of the process for handling invoices and credits. You should understand the system for granting authority for making purchases or paying invoices, documentation required to support payment requests, and the availability of special services such as the use of credit cards for purchases. If the library bills its staff time, services, or purchases to customers, this is the department that will handle those transactions. This is also the group that is responsible for maintaining appropriate financial controls to assure the protection of company assets. You should ask for documents or discussion to clarify the company's procedures for maintaining controls and handling financial transactions.

- *Training.* This group provides training both in the main areas of the company's business and in support areas. You should identify training courses that will apply to your work. These might include computer skills, management training, personal development (time management, writing, speaking), interpersonal relations, teamwork, etc. It is also important to understand what training is provided to the company staff and how the library can cooperate and support training efforts. For example, the library might house and circulate self-study materials, be the resource center for training materials, or maintain a supply of portable computers for use in training activities.

- *Computing environment.* In today's and tomorrow's library organizations, understanding the company's computing environment will be absolutely essential. Librarians will work within this environment to apply computer technology to information activities. Computing activities and technology may be centralized with an overall MIS group and a mainframe system or may be decentralized with MIS groups in each division and local- and wide-area networks or some combination of these. Areas to become familiar with immediately are hardware, software, networks and staff support availability, standards for hardware and software, processes for acquiring hardware and software and obtaining consulting services, computer resource security, and how costs are billed. Much has been written about the communication difficulties between systems people and librarians. An effort on the part of the librarian to understand how the systems staff work will go a long way toward eliminating these problems and forging effective alliances between the library and systems staff.

Button Pushers

In every company, at any given time, certain themes will elicit strong reactions. I call these "button pushers." Some currently popular themes are quality, safety, teamwork, diversity, interdependence, cost containment, and global thinking. In addition to these, each company will have its own "hot buttons" related to a product, a market, a customer, etc. Projects or activities attached to these themes will have precedence over others, will receive more enthusiastic support, and will more easily command resources. Aligning yourself with these themes will give you visibility and credibility. Conversely, ignoring or working against these themes not only will be frustrating, but will label you as someone who does not understand what the company values.

Behavioral Norms

Every company has a set of norms of behavior that is accepted and rewarded — the way successful employees are expected to behave. These behavioral norms may not be codified anywhere. They may not be uniformly practiced, and their existence may even be denied. Therefore, they can be elusive, but are very real, and play a major part in how employees are perceived. In the following paragraphs, I have given a few examples of the these norms. There are, of course, many more, but these will suffice as examples of the types of behavioral norms that affect how employees are perceived.

- *Work hours/work ethic.*   Most employees are told what their expected work hours are. These may apply to all employees alike, or there may be flexible work-hour systems. However, in many (maybe most) companies, professional employees, to be highly regarded, are expected to work more hours than those required. In some companies the eight or nine hour day may be what is expected. In others, the ten or eleven hour day is the norm with an occasional eighty-hour week. Librarians who have personal constraints that limit the time they can physically spend at the office may need to find ways to do work outside the office. Laptop computers, remote computer connections, and facsimile equipment are reducing the need to actually be in the office to accomplish tasks. Some progressive companies, seeking to foster a balance between work life and family life, discourage more than the normal work week, but that is not presently the prevalent ethic.

- *Dress code.*   Some companies have official dress codes, but if not, there is definitely an unofficial dress code. I feel strongly that librarians should be guided by how other administrative professionals dress. The degree of formality will vary from company to company, but the librarian will be more readily identified as part of the team if she or he conforms to whatever is perceived as appropriate dress for administrative professionals.

- *Writing style.* Each company develops a preferred writing style. This style is usually very different from the academic writing style. It tends to be straightforward with a standard vocabulary. It is often said, in jest of course, that executives cannot read more than one page. Effective writers develop styles that present all the key elements on one page with subsequent pages used for backup information, supporting documentation, appendixes, and attachments. If specific training in effective writing is not available, you should get suggestions from your mentor or find good model documents to emulate. The trick is to avoid being trite and clichéd while at the same time using a style that is comfortable and familiar to the reader. You should expect that when you prepare documents that will be widely distributed or that will be read at higher levels, they will be reviewed several times and revisions will be suggested. If you view these recommendations as a learning experience and do not allow "pride of authorship" to affect the way you receive suggestions, your writing style will improve.

- *Taking risks.* Some companies have a much higher tolerance for risk than others. Risk-taking tolerance also varies within the company according to the type of risk. In some companies, the axiom "Better to ask forgiveness than permission" holds true. In others, it does not, and employees who take actions without seeking supervisors' advice or approval will be perceived as using poor business judgment.

- *Chain of command.* Some companies expect employees to follow a very rigid chain of command with transactions handled at various levels in the organization depending on the type of transaction. Other companies have, or are moving toward, a more flexible approach where various units communicate across the organization rather than up and down it.

Corporate Character

Corporate America is in the process of reinventing itself. Technology, social change, and economic necessity are causing companies to reexamine their fundamental ways of doing business and select what to keep and what to change. It is a difficult task — change is never easy, and many companies have made changes only to find themselves worse off than before. However, the changes are essential if we are to compete in the global economy. Librarians, especially those in managerial positions, have exciting opportunities to participate in these changes. Because librarians become involved in so many different aspects of company business, and, if they take advantage of the opportunities, have such a wide network of contacts, they are well-positioned to become the "border guards" championed by Alan Wilkins in *Developing Corporate Character.*

> The concept of border guards is challenging. It does not suggest that subgroup character can be developed at will. It does, however, suggest that many people can be involved in developing organizational character, even if only in their own group. There is room for hope and for employees at all levels of the organization to contribute. They must, however, be astute. They must not miss cultural signals and political constraints. My most important message is that they must try.[1]

So, even as librarians accomplish the task of knowing the company and its business, they can embrace the even greater challenge of being agents for change for a better company.

References

1. Wilkins, Alan L. *Developing Corporate Character; How to Successfully Change an Organization Without Destroying It.* San Francisco: Jossey-Bass, 1989, pp. 129-30

Chapter 6
How to Talk to Senior Management
Susan A. Merry

If our goal is to manage the organization's information services, it will require information professionals to be assertive, aggressive, alert, and ambitious in their relationships with customers and vendors, but especially with senior management. Communicating with senior management may be easy or difficult, frequent or infrequent, stimulating or frightening, but one thing it is not, is an option.

If such communication seems a daunting task, it is probably because information professionals have labored in relative obscurity and isolation from senior management. We are mostly underexposed, unfamiliar, and hence uncomfortable in the executive board room. Additionally, we have operated through a long period of (relative) prosperity where performance measurement and productivity improvement were not a requirement of the culture. However, the workplace has changed permanently. Competition (external and internal) for our role now surrounds us, and organizations intent on survival are rightsizing and restructuring. We must recognize these two critical conditions. This is the best, but last, opportunity to educate senior management about our role and capabilities to manage the information services function for our organizations. If we miss this one, we will be looking for alternative careers.

In preparing to talk to senior management, we are going to consider four areas. First, we must understand the external environment and how it impacts our organization; second, the internal environment, our organization's culture and information needs; third, the credibility gap that separates us from senior management; and fourth, our performance, the standard of excellence we must achieve for survival.

The External Environment

Multiple forces are at work in the external environment. Are we aware of trends in the economic, social, and political environments that impact our organization's strategic direction? Are we alert to the organization's exposure to, or proclivity for, proposals from (information) consultants, brokers, or vendors? The information marketplace is now full of competitors, where originally (pre-electronic days?) it was almost exclusively ours. Do we aggressively review new products in this marketplace to determine their value for our operation?

We must own this responsibility and plan to incorporate electronic products and services as appropriate to our information strategy and organizational need. This task is difficult in a climate of cost constraint. It will require partners, external and internal, and endorsement by senior management, to execute. Nevertheless, it is (again) our responsibility to find and develop these partnerships, to be the organization's contact point, manage vendor contracts, and in partnership with our customers, win approval from senior management for our information strategy.

The Internal Environment

Policy and program changes that impact an organization at large are normally approved at a senior level. Information management policy and programs potentially impact an organization at large; therefore they require approval at a senior level. Because information is our business, we must be involved at this senior level.

Recognition of the value of information to an organization has improved dramatically over the past few years and will continue to grow. In a 1990 study of 150 leading companies in the United Kingdom, Peat Marwick Management Consultants found that when strategy was being determined or performance measured, "Use of external information is generally rare." People (competition and customers) and the marketplace (trade associations and conferences) are the most popular means of obtaining external information. The consultants, however, comment, "Failure to make use of external information ... suggests that many companies are trying to operate in a vacuum."[1]

Couple that with Peter Drucker's current view of the information revolution. "Information has always been power. ... The next 10 or 15 years are the years of moving from computer literacy to information literacy. ... Today, this idea of owning, or sharing, information means not only that the middle manager owns it or that the supervisor owns it. Everyone at every level owns it. Despite this necessity, expect the idea to be resisted."[2]

Technology consultant Robert Muir writes about the new learning organization: "Knowledge and time are the ultimate competitive business denominators of the nineties. ... Companies that thrive and survive in our global marketplace will be information-based."[3]

We must understand our organization's current view of information. Is information strategically valued? Are considerable (financial) resources available to support it, with a large customer base using it? Or is senior management largely unsupportive or unaware of the organization's level and volume of use of information products and services required in a competitive climate to keep the organization on the leading edge? The answer to this will help determine your starting point in developing and articulating a strategy for management to review.

New Parlance, New Paradigms

Consider the shifts: from proactive to partnership, from centralized access to desktop delivery, from standalone to networked, from intermediary to end-user support. Study the new vocabulary: process review, reengineering, outsourcing, learning organization, customer driven, knowledge workers, relationship management. You will think of other buzzwords appropriate to your particular environment (or check Stephen Abram's list in *Special Libraries*.[4]). Call this exercise a reference check to further measure where you and your organization are today.

Does your organization have a mission statement, updated goals and objectives, a clear strategic direction, a more rigorous performance measurement program? Is there an organization that has not adopted some form of "quality management"? Are you clear about this culture and alert to shifts within it? We cannot perform in a vacuum. We must tie our (information services) goals and objectives and strategies to those of the parent organization and we must articulate them in plain language. They form the basis of any presentation to senior management.

The new slant is "customer driven." This translates into the "next step" for information professionals. It offers the opportunity to build closer relationships with an already established customer base. Drucker[2] expressed concern that (some of) those holding information view it as power and are reluctant to share it, an attitude that will prevent an organization from achieving the competitive edge. Information professionals, on the other hand, are expressly trained to share information, and thus have an extraordinary opportunity to expand their role as information consultants, to become partners with key customer groups, and to push to participate in planning sessions, task forces, projects, i.e., wherever there is an information component.

Conflicting with this opportunity, however, is the challenge of matching the (still) increasing cost of information products and services to a prolonged and pervasive program of cost reduction within most organizations. This calls for a review and reassessment of your present information strategies. Some form of survey of your customers is required to identify and rank the value of your products and services. The cost of these strategies will be a further determinant of their acceptance. Therefore, expect to be challenged on your chargebacks, cost allocations, or fee-for-service policies. Recognize (accept) that a sharper focus will be placed on the "need to have" strategies, while the "nice to have" may have to be eliminated.

Capitalize on your access to competitive information on comparable or best-practice libraries. Collect it, swap it and, assuming that your performance is comparable, plan to present it to demonstrate your cost-effectiveness, i.e., that your cost is comparable to or better than those of competitors. Management likes such benchmarks.

Management also likes outsourcing functions that improve the bottom line. Learn what it would cost to outsource all or parts of your operation. You may be surprised. If access, timeliness, competitiveness, and confidentiality factor into the equation, and your operation is cost-effective as measured by you and accepted by your customers, there is no gain in outsourcing the organization's information services. However, management may assume otherwise until you present the facts. You want to prove that it would be false economy to outsource or reduce access to information. Access to information leads to better-informed decisions.

The Credibility Gap

Have you heard any of the following? "But they're only librarians" ... "I didn't know they did that" ... "I didn't know you had this" ... "You call what you do, research?" ... "How would you know what I need?" Such comments are neither complimentary to nor comprehending of the information professional's capacity, knowledge, judgment, or experience, which in combination offers a powerful package in fulfillment of all of the above. Where have we gone wrong? Why are we not considered automatically today as essential partners on various planning and project teams, task forces, or any organizational undertaking with an information resource component? Not to be too disparaging, a few among us have made it, perhaps even as (real) CIOs (Chief Information Officers), but in the main, we labor as middle managers, vulnerable and threatened in a prolonged period of downsizing and decreasing budgets.

An organization that understands and accepts the growing centrality of information in planning, competitive analysis, and decision-making, or the need to be first, best, or on the leading edge is an organization that is unlikely to eliminate its internal information center, especially one that has demonstrated its cost-effectiveness, impact, and customer satisfaction.

Our task, then, is to close whatever credibility gap exists. Remember, it is not with our customers that we lack credibility. It is with decision-makers, often found in the upper financial ranks, whose information needs are satisfied largely by numbers, as used in performance measurement, forecasts, ratios, and profitability models. This group needs to be educated about our business and persuaded about our value. In turn, we must accept and adopt the techniques used by senior management to manage operational expense. We must apply our statistics to measure or quantify the value they represent. We must benchmark our activities against those of best-practice companies in our own or other businesses. We must present the facts on outsourcing. Above all, we must survey our customers, solicit their input on our products and services, get their endorsement, and take their feedback up the line. Armed with all this we must be assertive, even aggressive, in gaining approval for our strategies as high up in the organization as is required. It is our job to do that, to close the credibility gap.

In her study "The Impact of the Special Library on Corporate Decision-Making"[5], Joanne Marshall surveyed 390 managers and executives (a statistically valid sampling from a population of 2,000) in five financial institutions in Toronto. Her goal was to assess the value of information provided by the five libraries and the impact it had on executive behavior. Her results are most appropriately used with senior management, and the overheads included in the report can be used in a presentation to demonstrate that the library is a valuable corporate asset.

Here are some examples of her results. The quality of information provided was rated 87% accurate and current, 89% timely, and 72.2% relevant. The cognitive value of the information (contribution to the knowledge of the manager or executive) was measured as providing new knowledge in 87.6% of cases. Furthermore, 86.3% of respondents stated that the information provided was of value in their particular decision-making situation; 83.9% led to better-informed decisions and 73.2% led to increased confidence in the decision. More than half (54.5%) of the participants handled some aspect of their decision-making differently as a result of the information provided. Further impact was assessed under the avoidance of negative outcomes for the organization: avoiding a poor business decision 74.6%, preventing loss of own time, 67.9%, or another person's time 66.2%. Next highest ratings were prevention of loss of funds 57.8%, and loss of a client 40.1%.

These results provide compelling evidence of the value the information professional brings to corporate decision-making. Further, the managers and executives participating in this survey represented the core business of the industry studied (banking). Being suppliers to the core business and to executive management is exactly what we want, because it enhances the information professional's credibility and visibility, and both are needed. If you are not now suppliers to your core business, you are vulnerable. You must concentrate your "need to have" services on strategically targeted customer groups.

A second source of documentation particularly potent for dialogue with senior management is provided by José-Marie Griffiths and Donald W. King in their study *Special Libraries: Increasing the Information Edge*[6]. This work summarizes and presents evidence accumulated from 27 independent studies (10,000 statistical survey responses) to demonstrate the usefulness, value, and worth of organization libraries. It confirms that

> documents provided through organization libraries and information services,
> contribute substantially more to the quality and productivity than documents
> from other sources. Further, that professionals who extensively use their

organization libraries perform their work considerably better and faster than those who do not. This relative advantage or gain that can be achieved through effective use of information and libraries is what we refer to as the information edge.

Working with your own numbers — e.g., population served by various services, estimated salary (value) of your average customer, salary (cost) of your average information professional, total cost of operating the library and each major product or service, (e.g., circulation or routing service, acquisition expenses, online costs) — you can measure your performance. Analyze these unit costs, the dollar value derived from library services and the ratio of value to cost (costbenefit). The results will demonstrate the advantages of supporting a centralized in-house library and information service. However, because outsourcing is currently so attractive a concept to management, it is critical to be able to demonstrate your cost-effectiveness and the alternative higher prices paid to acquire information without a library. Because senior management, removed from the core activities you perform, are likely to assume that the organization could do without its library-as-cost-center, the data you compile on these issues and the managerial skill you demonstrate by doing so could mean the difference between survival and extinction.

Excelling Within the Structure

"Making a difference," developing "win-win" strategies, and achieving "recognition for excellence" are not easy in today's environment. And we will not do it alone. We will accomplish our goal in partnership with our customers, our external suppliers (publishers, information product and database producers, software vendors), and our internal suppliers (of hardware and software platforms and communications facilities). Information professionals must drive this link between customers and suppliers. Consultant Stephen Arnold suggests that "creating partnerships requires a business plan, excellent implementation skills, and salesmanship. Without any one of these key ingredients, the library's goals are likely to be difficult, if not impossible, to reach."[7]

Vehicles for Presentation to Senior Management

Your reporting structure can help or hinder you in reaching senior management. The desirable structure is of course to report to the executive level and to one who is versed in information management issues. If this is not the case, then finding a champion, a mentor, your most strategically placed customer, or some combination of the above may be what you need to access the decision-makers and present your case and credentials.

In presentations to senior management, the format, the timetable, and the audience appropriate to the task are all a factor of your culture. If your organization favors an annual planning cycle, request permission to present your plans at that time. If your manager has regular meetings with a senior finance executive or committee (whoever controls your budget), propose that you attend a meeting to discuss with that executive or group new initiatives, funding alternatives, or competitive products required.

You must expect and accept that senior management do not know your business or your jargon. Do not use it. Use language common to management and financial discussion; be clear and concise; offer solutions not problems. If your audience is composed of non-customers, take samples of a brochure, bibliography, newsletter, or whatever marketing tools you use. Start your presentation with your goals and objectives, carefully connected to those of the organization. Use overheads to present information that lends itself to graphic display. Illustrate your discussion of services with examples of success stories. (We all have them!) Be prepared to leave an information package (summary form) with your audience. Stick to your allotted timeframe but allow for questions. If you cannot answer a question posed to you, confirm that you will get back with the answer. This is your time to make an impact; make the most of it!

What an enormous challenge we face today as information professionals! If we are ambitious enough, we will seize the opportunity. Consider this: your organization has had access to electronic information for almost two decades, and it has been delivered mainly through the library. You have formed, over the years, key relationships and developed core competencies in serving your customers. You are now well acquainted with the organization's needs and the vendor community. You have devoted more time than probably anyone else in your organization to the study of all aspects of the information marketplace, including its future. Knowing what you do, you should welcome the opportunity to manage your customers' information needs and to sell senior management on your ability to do that. You understand that too much information is available, but you know how to access it, which sources are appropriate to your information need, and how to put further controls on incoming data with filters and profiles. You alone understand what is available and affordable or appropriate for your customers for desktop delivery, and what is not. You now have the opportunity to manage the three-way partnership of supplier, end user, and information professional. If we understand these deliverables, and can manage their implementation, we will unquestionably be "making a difference."

The Chief Information Officer role has been won in the past by systems professionals, data processing experts, versed largely in mainframe technology, who understand this technology well but have little understanding of "information." A more accurate title would be Chief Technology Officer. The information professional, on the other hand, has always understood that "information" not "technology" is the strategic resource, also that this information is not necessarily technology driven. The better choice for CIO today would be someone from the ranks of information professionals experienced in both internal and external information management, who are supported by technology and focused on the customer. As Laurence Prusak and James Matarazzo succinctly put it:

> Information Management is sometimes confused with Information Technology and/or Information Systems. Information Technologies are the physical resources used to manipulate information. While these technologies have transformed the various ways information can be acquired, stored, retrieved and distributed, they still remain fundamentally an enabling tool for the management of information. Technology itself neither produces, evaluates, understands nor adds meaning to information.[8]

Today's Tools, Tomorrow's Triumphs

In this chapter we have tried to assess the current environment, our capabilities, and the obstacles to be overcome to gain credibility and establish a necessary alliance with senior management. In summary, we have to demonstrate leadership and accountability, increase access to information, maintain responsibility for its management, and control the overall cost of doing so. If we can achieve this, we should claim ownership of the organization's information services function. Then we will be recognized by senior management as team players and essential partners in today's learning organization and beyond.

References

1. Information for Strategic Management; A Survey of Leading Companies, 1990. Commissioned by KPMG Peat Marwick Management Consultants from the Harris Research Center. (Out of print. Access by interlibrary loan.)

2. "According to Peter Drucker," Forbes ASAP, March 29, 1993, pp. 90-95.

3. Muir, Robert F. "Marketing your Library or Information Service to Business." Online, 17(4), July 1993, pp. 41-46.

4. Abram, Stephen. "Buzzwords for 2005," Special Libraries, Fall 1993, p. 216.

5. Marshall, Joanne. The Impact of the Special Library on Corporate Decision-Making. Final report of a research project funded by the Special Libraries Association. Washington, D.C., 1993.

6. Griffiths, J.M., and D.W. King. Special Libraries: Increasing the Information Edge. Washington, D.C.: Special Libraries Association, 1993. 191 p.

7. Arnold, Stephen. "Relationships of the Future: Vendors and Partners" *Special Libraries* 84(4), fall 1993, pp. 235-40.

8. Prusak, Laurence, and James Matarazzo. *Information Management and Japanese Success*. Washington, D.C.: Special Libraries Association and Ernst and Young, 1992.

Chapter 7
Getting to the Right Answer
Beth Duston

> ...a little knowledge is dangerous. ...
> —Thomas Huxley, 1877

In today's supercompetitive environment, access to relevant information often becomes the determining factor for successful decision-making. Corporations and individuals alike are faced with information choices that are increasing exponentially. In 1900, the entire body of information in the world was doubling every 100 years. Today the amount of information doubles every 21 months. Each day the U.S. government and businesses alone generate 900 million pages of information. Electronic access to and the processing of information has become absolutely necessary to cope with the amount of information available today.

In addition to these new information sources, the information applications emerging today are not based on a single technology, or on a single media format. They are an interesting blend of several, including local-area networks, wide-area networks, CD-ROMs, magnetic tapes, dial-in access, online services and many others. These new technologies are providing more opportunities for the end user to find his own answer with menu-driven databases that are easy to use and do not require the services of an intermediary. Networked CD-ROMs allow users to search in the comfort of their offices without being charged a fee for time logged on the system or the database. Customized electronic newsletters, providing only the information of interest to the user, are becoming increasingly popular. Bulletin boards on the Internet and other information systems allow users to interact instantly with other professionals around the world.

The information intermediary is confronted daily with these new changes, and the evolving information landscape is presenting new horizons and challenges for the information provider. The highways providing new information sources and the new travelers on those information superhighways require information specialists who are well informed about the new landscape, who understand the new technologies as well as the information sources, and who can assist and guide these new travelers in the right direction to the best answer.

Providing answers to questions is becoming more challenging. Getting the right answer to a question is similar to taking a drink of water from a hydrant—take too much and you drown; take too little and you may not get the right or best answer. Filtering, synthesizing, and packaging information must be directed toward providing usable knowledge for the user.

Regardless of the new methods in information transmission and distribution, the information seeker must have confidence and trust in the information provider. The customer expects to have the same respect for his privacy and confidentiality about his questions and answers as he expects from his physician or lawyer. He must feel absolutely confident with the information provider in order to communicate sensitive or awkward questions. A scientist, engineer, or market analyst might be reluctant to admit that he needs help and be nervous about sharing questions with a colleague, let alone with a stranger. With very little interaction, the information provider might be able to determine whether the request is for a new product, patent, court case, or trademark infringement.

Since questions and answers often are confidential, the information specialist must treat all customers fairly and equitably. Occasionally a new client will require a confidentiality agreement from the information provider. Several years ago, the president of a new enterprise requested information and required that such an agreement be signed. His firm had received tremendous venture capital backing and he was racing to complete his product before the competitors did. Every person from the company who interacted with the information specialist was given the same confidentiality assurances and respect.

Because of these concerns with confidentiality, senior managers in some large corporations do not use the services of their own corporate information center and external information brokers are asked to provide the requested information. In certain cases this is because managers are not as concerned about the risks using external information specialists as they are that the librarian will share their information with other departments. The fierce competition that exists between departments, particularly in periods of downsizing, creates fiefdoms in large corporations. The information specialist must have the sensitivity and the savvy to know when or when not to share information, even within a corporation. This understanding and confidence often takes many years to establish.

Trust is also gained by being honest about the subject material. A person with a broken ankle does not go to a dentist for assistance; likewise a person does not expect an information specialist with a legal background to understand chemical formulations. Librarians and information brokers usually are very eager to be helpful in providing a customer with service. However, if the right resource is not consulted, a little wrong information is certainly worse than no information at all. For example, in order to search a British database it is necessary to know the British spellings or terms for the items being searched, such as "spanner" instead of "wrench". A person retrieving a few items under "fiber optics" might conclude the search without ever considering the more common British "fibre optics."

Not only is it important for the subject specialist to be aware of the traditional sources of information but he or she must know the new sources as well. What are the new bulletin boards on the Internet? Are there new subject-specific journals? new databases? or even new employees with specific subject expertise? It is far better for the information provider to admit a limited knowledge of a particular subject than to proceed, and an offer to find a subject specialist to assist the user can often be as valuable as finding the specific answer. The information provider must never, never let the customer leave the library or the office dissatisfied. That person's needs must be met with either quality answers or quality guidance.

The reliability of the information is also important. How often does that directory get updated? Is the information comprehensive enough? Since the goal is to provide the best answer for each question, it is important that the sources searched be accurate and current. To answer that, the information specialist must be well informed about current sources. Reading professional and subject-specialty journals, attending seminars and conferences, and being able to access new technologies with new information sources are essential and critical in promoting customer trust. And while attendance at library and information science meetings is important, it is equally important for the information provider to attend subject-specialty meetings of groups, for example the American

Chemical Society or Institute of Electrical and Electronics Engineers, if those are the subjects of his or her work.

Information needs within a corporation vary according to frequency, subject, and source consulted. Information audits and information needs assessments have repeatedly shown that employees rely on internal information sources about 80 percent of the time and external sources about 20 percent of the time. The knowledge that a colleague may have the answer to a question is actually more valuable than the most comprehensive collection of external information. Research has shown that 80 percent of the questions are completely or partially answered on the first query. For questions that can be answered simply or easily, it is usually enough to have <u>an</u> answer, not necessarily spending a great amount of time searching for the best answer. Often it is sufficient for a colleague or professional to point the employee in the right direction so that he can proceed with this work.

Employees and clients typically seek answers from an information specialist or information broker because they are stuck; they cannot get the answer from their traditional sources, and cannot do their work without an answer. If the results from the first query are unfruitful or disappointing, a simple search in external information, i.e., a book or an online service or a journal, usually yields an answer. Similarly, the comprehensive literature search can be another type of information request requiring external information and is especially useful if the employee or client is just embarking on a new area of technical or marketing research and needs to get up to speed with the subject or technology of the subject.

Reference Interview

The quality of the answer is directly proportional to the quality of the question.

The first step that the information specialist must take in determining a client's research needs is a reference interview. Information specialists identify information requests using a combination of open-ended and close-ended questions. Customers are encouraged to respond at length in order to elaborate on their information needs. Questions should be prefaced with such words as what, when, who, why, where, and how.

Asking questions is a skill, and unfortunately one in which many adults fail miserably. Sometimes it is assumed that the searcher intuitively knows the information needs of the researcher. Also the researcher, especially a scientist or engineer, may be embarrassed or uncomfortable that he does not know the answer. Several years ago a researcher requested information about artificial intelligence. It was not at all clear what type of information he required. As he slowly answered questions in the reference interview, it became clear that he actually wanted a biweekly update from *Commerce Business Daily* specifically on how the federal government was spending its research dollars on artificial intelligence since he wanted to use that information for his long-range corporate strategic plan. If the government spent research dollars on certain research initiatives, this client wanted to know about it. From his initial query, alone, however, it was impossible to anticipate the direction of the research.

Not only does technology change rapidly, so does the language that describes the technology. The term "maser" preceded the term "laser," for example. Each database indexes its citations in different ways, so it is very difficult to undertake a comprehensive search with all possible synonyms. One approach to overcoming this problem is to request from the researcher a paper or group of papers which he may have consulted and which closely reflect the type and kind of answer or research desired. It is much easier and cheaper to search a particular paper on the author or title field than to try to anticipate all synonyms, descriptors, identifiers, classification codes, or products that are used in a given database.

As a general rule, if the scope of the research is rather broad and there are no known research papers to use as examples, recommending approximately twenty titles to the client is a good initial step. Titles, particularly in the sciences, usually reflect quite accurately the substance of the research, so the client can then advise the information specialist whether any of the titles are appropriate or whether the search must be further refined.

In some subjects, an older paper that is considered to be a classic can also be useful in producing good current research answers, and a quick search in *Science Citation Index* will provide current citations to the older research. Conversely, if a scientist wants to know how *his* research papers are being cited and any new applications of his research, a search of this database, or in the case of patents, a search of the *Claims-Citation* database, may provide answers.

Once a client has determined which titles will probably yield the best answers, a presentation format must be decided upon for the final product and the information provider must ask several questions. Will an abstract be enough? Is full text or full image needed? Is the actual document required?

Information specialists provide better answers to questions when they are familiar with the research tools used. No one person can fully understand the nuances of more than fifteen databases of the hundreds available. If there is an equivalent paper resource, e.g. Chemical Abstracts, and it is considered a quality information resource, it undoubtedly will have a quality online version. Many vendors, capitalizing on the information explosion, are developing new products which can be subsets of these quality resources.

It is important for the information specialist to understand the objective of the search. What does the client want to do with the information? Is it a market research question? Does the requestor need to know a technology as it relates to market research or to engineering? Understanding how the information will be used helps in selecting the most useful databases for that search. Is the research ongoing or is the client ready to file a patent? If the latter is the case, it must be recognized that most information contained in patent databases never is found elsewhere and the "language" of the patent often does not resemble the language for references in the "open" literature. In addition, searching patent databases often can provide insight into new corporate developments.

In some cases, of course, the researcher may provide certain restraints to the search. Information may be restricted to the last few years, in the English language only and only in journal articles. For example, the citations of a rather prolific author may not be desired by the researcher and so not be included in the search.

Finally, the information specialist must ask when the information is needed. Fortunately, not every researcher needs the answer "yesterday." If at all possible, he or she should decide with the researcher on a satisfactory date and time for delivery.

Producing the Answer

If this is the first interaction between the information provider and the researcher, the first decision has to do with the delivery of the information—whether it will be transmitted by mail, private courier, fax, modem, or e-mail. Most people are creatures of habit and, if satisfied with a particular format, will continue and expect to ask for and receive information in the same way.

I typically provide literature searches in a landscape (sideways) format. One day for convenience, I chose a portrait format. The researcher was distressed and thought that he was getting less satisfactory information because of this change in format! He was assured that it was the same information presented in a different configuration, but nonetheless, the report was redone in the landscape format.

For a paper format, I usually bind the final report in a spiral binder using a landscape format with wide margins for comments and notes. The cover lists the nature of the search and databases used in the search. A page outlining the search strategy is included, which is useful if the researcher wants to perform a similar search at a later date or if he wants the searcher to keep the search updated.

If the final report is free of misspellings, online noise, duplicates, "miss hits," and the like, the transaction will result in a more professional product. Because so many end users perform their own searches, using an information intermediary must provide obvious, tangible value-added enhancements in order for the researcher to be satisfied.

A follow-up call should be placed several days after delivering the information. This is especially important with a new client, for if the search has not yielded the right results, the call will provide an opportunity to discuss any problems or difficulties and/or any follow-on searches.

Furthermore, an evaluation form should be included with the final product. This is useful to determine whether the service was satisfactory and whether the correct databases were used, and to obtain suggestions for other formats and for future products and services. Favorable comments can be used for future references.

If the product and service have produced a happy and satisfied researcher, he will continue to seek the services of the information intermediary. The satisfaction that comes to the information intermediary from guiding the researcher to the right answer cannot be measured.

Chapter 8
Corporate Libraries: A Soft Analysis, A Warning, and Some Generic Advice
Laurence Prusak

Corporate libraries, after a few decades of moderate growth, began to really take off during the 1950s. They were first established, and continued to operate, on a set of principles not at all dissimilar to those that were developed earlier for public libraries. These can be roughly summarized as follows.

- Information is an abstract, but self-evident, "good" in itself.
- Giving access to information will somehow improve the productivity (or, in the case of public libraries, civic-mindedness) of the potential end user of this information.
- Library operations need to be managed using a unique set of tools, methods, and a body of knowledge that needs to be taught at a graduate level.

By a great stroke of fortune (at least, for the library community), these three principles were greatly re-enforced and amplified by the concurrent explosive growth of the development and use of computers. This, in turn, brought with it an extraordinary accompanying rhetoric surrounding the widely trumpeted Information Age.

Although computers were made commercially available in the early 1950s, their widespread adoption really gained force starting in the early 1960s. Nevertheless, computerization had a powerful influence on how business thought about information and its management. In turn this influenced the reasons corporate libraries were established and how they were evaluated by their corporate patrons. It is worth looking further into this powerful influence in order to better understand how corporate libraries and librarians arrived at their current problematic state. Three particular developments are worth discussing here.

The first development is the notion that librarians, and the concepts they are taught, tend to view information as a "thing."[1] This perspective leads one to view information as passive — that it can be managed in a way similar to the way one manages other "passive" assets or "things." This passive "thingness" view of information naturally leads to evaluating success as a quantitative valuation of retrieval "hits" rather than judgment and responsibility toward the information usage. Based as it is on concepts developed for managing *computerized* and programmable information, this concept absolves the manager and deliverer of information for responsibility concerning the information's quality and ultimate value to the user. It has increased the value of the storage and retrieval of information as it decreases the human skill of evaluating the information's value. The aim is to identify information *materials* by key words, rather than seeking the *best* information available to help managers make sense out of a situation. The responsibility for evaluating "bestness," which involves a level of expertise and skills not often associated with corporate libraries, nor taught at most library schools, remains up for grabs in the corporate marketplace.

A second factor, also strongly influenced by Information Age rhetoric, is the confusion extant within the business community between the machinery that manipulates information (computers, software, etc.) and the information itself. Within many firms it is assumed, however false this picture may be, that the information technology (IT) organization, having the word "information" in its title, therefore is responsible for information provision, quality, and relevance within the organization. This assumption is quite pernicious, since the IT organization usually manages only about 10 percent of the potentially useful information within most organizations and has little or no interest in the unstructured information world. Within many organizations, this lack of interest in the great mass of nonstructured information has led to a strong sense of dissatisfaction with the IT organizations and their usurpation of information within their title. Ironically, just as many firms are turning away from a technology-led information polity, many librarians have vigorously jumped upon this very technology bandwagon as a source of ideas about what firms need in the way of information services.

It is very clear that many managers and executives do not receive, through computer systems, the information they need to run their businesses.[2] Given this situation it would seem that libraries could step in and become the acknowledged function providing highly valued, noncomputer-structured information. Examples of these information categories are internal expertise, competitive information, and client information. The fact that this has not happened with any frequency brings us to our third factor.

This factor is perhaps less tangible than the other two but no less real. It concerns how librarians identify themselves, their roles within corporations, and how they perceive the value they bring to their organizations. Like other professionals, librarians, and the professional literature they learn from, have a defined-role self-image. These mental models that we all possess are powerful impetuses to action, and individuals will go to often extraordinary lengths to defend their self-image.

When we look at the collective self-image of librarians we find that they have two central components: undifferentiated service and a strong bias toward a contingency approach to information acquisition and distribution. Unfortunately, these two attitudes are countercultural in most businesses today. To try to maintain universal service in this age of dramatic downsizing and margin pressures seems doomed from the start and is being abandoned by most other corporate functions. Yet many corporate librarians burn the midnight oil struggling to continue serving everyone, even with cut budgets and severely reduced headcounts. There are very, very few useful things one can do with information in serving a client-base of several thousand. Yet this is precisely the position of many corporate librarians. As far as the warehouse[3] mode of information storage (be it warehoused on disks or actual hard copy), this, too, is drastically inappropriate in a just-in-time world. Far better would be to acknowledge, as Peter Drucker proclaims, that every manager should be responsible for his or her individual information management and have the librarian become an internal consultant in helping them achieving this end.

Where, then, does this leave corporate librarians? For one thing, it seems clear they need to carve out a specific niche for themselves based on their demonstrated and historical specific competencies. They then need to demonstrate the value of these competencies to those who pay the bills.

The following generic approach might be of value in rethinking how a corporate librarian can bring new value to his or her organization. Clearly, all such exercises as this one are strongly contextual and can have very different outcomes in different organizations. However, this analysis and set of suggestions may help librarians play to their own strengths while exploiting the weaknesses of the other internal groups that compete for internal resources on the basis of managing information. Although this notion of groups competing for ever scarcer resources may be antithetical to most librarians, it is nevertheless a truism in corporate life. This generic approach can be effectively divided into four steps.

Step 1. Decide what unit, division, function, process, or strategic business unit you wish to work with in helping them manage information. In other words, draw a boundary around the group you want to help. Working for the entire enterprise (if it is bigger than a few hundred people) positions you as a low-value commodity-based utility. However, you should choose your group, and its executives, with great care. Try to find a group with executives who have a clear need for varied information combined with an orientation that allows them to appreciate and value information as a worthy resource. In particular, it makes much sense to sell your value exclusively to the group's senior executives. You may need to abandon universal service concepts while first attempting to establish your value with a new group.

Step 2. Get to know and understand the actual work individuals do within this group. This can be done by in-depth interviews, focus groups, informal discussions, "free-lunch" meetings, etc. Remember that *you* will have to learn the vocabulary, frame of reference, and meaning context of your group. *They* will not learn *yours*. You might want to develop a framework, which will help you conceptualize these work tasks.

Step 3. The next step is to figure out what information would add value to the work of the group you analyzed. It is here that library-like skills can shine, especially in mapping what specific information can bringvalue to the group's work that the group currently does not get. If one takes responsibility for the information in terms of quality, relevance, and value, this too will bring plaudits. If possible, provide the information itself (or very easy access to it). It is also useful to keep in mind two propositions that are relevant here: (1) people do not know what they do not know so this task requires considerable creativity, and (2) many people are reluctant to display their ignorance, especially to people they perceive as junior to them.

Step 4. Spend time with individuals in your group. Learn their concerns, their "mission-critical" projects; their business environment; their aspirations, languages, and masters. Change your service offerings, as best you can, to coincide with burning agenda issues, while trying to build a *core* service that is more stable. Read the "standard" texts that *they* have read; subscribe to and read their key journals.

While this prescription is obviously schematic, it attempts to play to the proven strengths of librarians. Within a corporate setting, in an increasingly hostile environment, this exercise should provide some pointers toward a new approach to providing information services that will be continually valued.

References

1.   Buckland, Michael K. "Information as a Thing," *Journal of the American Society for Information Science*, 42(5), 1991, pp. 351-60.
2.   McKinnon, Sharon, and William Bruns Jr., *Information Mosaic*. Boston: Harvard Business School Press, 1992.
3.   Davenport, Thomas, and Laurence Prusak, "Blow Up the Corporate Library," *International Journal of Information Management*, 13(6), December 1993, pp. 405-12.

Chapter 9
SLA's Research Program:
Key for the Profession
Tobi A. Brimsek

There is little argument that the field of library and information science is an underresearched discipline. As the rapidly changing information society develops, there is no doubt that research can serve as a basis for setting policy and direction in information management. The importance of research rests not only in the data collection processes and analysis but in the use and interpretation of those data as an investment in understanding the events occurring in the evolution of the information-based society.

You might ask, so what? How does research impact on the average practitioner in the special libraries, or even broader, the information community? Just as a research proposal needs to be evaluated in a myriad of ways, ultimately it needs to pass the "so what" test. Similarly, the importance of research can be stated and espoused, but in terms of the bottom line, the impact of library and information research needs to be interpreted in terms of its usefulness to the profession. That usefulness may take a number of diverse forms such as a methodology which can serve as a model of best practices or benchmarking, an impact on determining the value of information products and services, or in the broadest sense, a way to help information professionals be most effective.

For some time the Special Libraries Association (SLA) has seen the importance of the role of research in its members' professional lives. A brief history reveals that SLA re-established a standing Research Committee in June 1988. This action was preceded by the creation of a position for a director of research, effective in January of that same year. By June 1989, the research program gained momentum as the Board of Directors approved the Research Agenda (see Figure 1 on page 90). As stated by Miriam Drake, then the SLA Research Committee Chair, "Priorities for the research agenda focus on what special librarians don't know but need to know in order to improve performance of libraries, information centers, and information professionals."[1]

The Association's renewed interest in research stemmed from the need to provide the data and analysis from which practical applications could be sought. The resurgence of the program underscores the critical need felt in the community about the role of research and the relationship of research results to job performance and growth. Once SLA established its new research program, actions of the Board of Directors continued to support the imperative need for this work in a 1988 Board action by naming research as one of the priorities in the Association's strategic plan.

Although the establishment of the research program formalized a set of activities and actions within the Association, the program had a number of previously existing components in place to fall under its aegis. One of the unifying components of preexisting aspects of the program with the new directions was the development and approval of a research agenda focusing on researchable questions of interest and importance to the special libraries community.

The biennial salary survey is a prime example of preexisting efforts, having been conducted in some form since 1959 (excluding the years 1960 to 1966). It has provided a wealth of salary and related data. In 1985 the first membership survey was conducted, the results of which provided significant and solid information on the demographics of the membership as well as the products and services of the Association that were being used and sought after by the members. In fact, the additions of the research program and a research position were some of the changes resulting, in part, from the survey research. Clearly, the course and case for research within the Association was set from the mid-1980s.

In 1986, Frank Spaulding, then SLA president, appointed a presidential task force, chaired by James Matarazzo, Simmons College. The task Force's purpose was to define "the value of the information professional." The report issued in June 1987 documented the approach to the problem of demonstrating the value of the information professional via three methodologies:

- measuring time—and its monetary equivalent—saved by information;
- determining real savings, financial gains, or liability avoidance; and
- assessing the worth of qualitative, anecdotal evidence.[2]

The report approached some of the basic questions that were to be blended into the future SLA Research Agenda. In fact, item 3.4 of the SLA Research Agenda asks, "What is the relationship between library/information services and corporate or institutional success?" This question relates directly to one of the recommendations of the task force report: "Continued research should be built on this foundation. The future of the information professional depends on their ability to clearly and persuasively justify their position in the corporation."[3]

These examples, as well as examination of a portion of Association history, serve to set the stage for some of the projects and approaches resulting from funding through the research program. It is also noteworthy that the Special Programs Fund was another preexisting grant program that was incorporated into the research program. Its purpose in funding projects having a broad applicability to the special libraries community fits well with the overall intent of the research program. As a result, a number of Special Programs Fund grant recipients have made salient contributions to the profession's core of knowledge. Specifically, the work on valuing corporate libraries by James M. Matarazzo along with Laurence Prusak and Michael Gautier was a direct outgrowth of the President's task force on the Value of the Information Professional. The survey conducted by these three researchers was in direct response to a recommendation by the Task Force for a study of the value placed by senior executives on the information professional as well as on the corporate library/information center.

The conclusions of that research were most significant.

- Librarians evaluate their performance based on standardized library methodologies. Their managers use far different, often subjective, evaluation criteria.
- There is little managerial consensus on how the library adds specific value to the firm's performance or how value should be measured.
- Librarians have little say on the firm's information policies and mission. Few respondents could state what exact function the library performs within the firm's information structure.
- Growing end-user usage of database systems and other information technologies will have a serious impact on business operations as well as on the role of the library within the firm.

Will the librarian perform as purchasing agent, gatekeeper, network manager, internal trainer, information specialist, or chief information officer? Librarians and their managers have done very little planning on this critical issue.

- There is still a strong reservoir of goodwill and affection for the library and librarians—often based on an intuitive "feel" that the service is valuable and worthy of continued support. However, in the increasingly volatile business climate, it is questionable whether libraries can grow based on these forms of approval. Considerable work must be done to ensure future growth![4]

Prusak and Matarazzo continued their investigations in the corporate arena with a study, *Information Management and Japanese Success*. This work, published in 1992, had as its objective

> to identify the characteristics of the Japanese approach to acquiring, managing, and disseminating the kinds of information they deemed critical to the success of their businesses. It was our hope to be able to provide insight into their information environment so that western companies with varying information needs could find creative approaches to their information management problems from among the companies...profiled...[5]

Six findings were brought forward from Prusak's and Matarazzo's work:

- Japanese firms place a tremendous value on information and do not feel the need to justify information management expenditures.
- Business information, events, and situations are perceived and presented in their contextual settings.
- The mission of the information function is closely aligned with the strategic thrust of the organization.
- Technology is seen as an enabler for information management, not the primary component.
- The management of the information function is rotated among all company managers.
- Japanese management reads.

The importance of this second study is to illustrate Japanese techniques which may be conceptually adopted by American companies as they reach out into the global marketplace. The juxtaposition of the two studies on the corporate sector provides yet a broader foundation for research activity in the special libraries community. Each of these studies has contributed to the growth of a knowledge base in need of expansion. The first related directly to value, the second more closely to the environment.

In 1991 the Special Libraries Association awarded a research grant to Joanne G. Marshall, associate professor, Faculty of Library and Information Science, University of Toronto. The nature of this grant dealt once again with the issue of value. The information environment has continued to offer a demanding challenge to information professionals in terms of being able to quantify their value. Marshall's survey involved the random selection of 390 managers and executives from five major financial institutions. The participants were used to determine the impact of the special library on corporate decision-making. There were five significant results.

- Better-informed decision-making was reported by 84 percent of the 299 managers and executives who returned their questionnaires.
- The special libraries were particularly effective in supplying new knowledge in decision-making situations and in increasing the level of confidence of managers and executives in the decisions being made.
- As a result of reading the information from the library, 54 percent of the respondents said that they probably or definitely handled some aspect of the decision-making situation differently from the way they would have handled it otherwise.
- The results showed that, when libraries are used in decision-making situations, the information provided is frequently perceived by the managers and executives as having a significant impact on their actions.
- In the current economic climate, the rapid delivery of accurate and up-to-date information was seen as more important than ever.[6]

The final report of Marshall's study referred to above was produced so that the methodology could serve as a model for other information professionals who wish to replicate the study. The significance of this type of work is clear—not only were there some very revealing results from the Marshall study, but also a tool for use by special librarians has been developed. Another stepping-stone to a fundamental research issue has been created.

In 1992 another major research study was funded by an SLA research grant. José-Marie Griffiths and Donald King published a book with their results, *Special Libraries: Increasing the Information Edge*. The book was written to provide special librarians with a system of measures for decision-making, ammunition for defending library budgets and competing for funds in an increasingly competitive environment. In the authors' words, "The purpose of this book is to summarize and present accumulated evidence of the usefulness, value, and impact of information, and of the contribution that the organization libraries make to the benefits gained from its use."[7] The results presented in the book relate to the "information edge" held by professionals through the use of information. The information edge is "the relative gain that can be accomplished through effective use of information by individuals, their organizations and their countries. The value of organization libraries and information centers ... is that they can fulfill specific needs and satisfy certain requirements better and less expensively than any other alternative."[8]

The very scope and breadth of the work by Griffiths and King define its usefulness. They "approached the question of usefulness, value and impact of information and libraries from a variety of perspectives, and found confirming evidence of positive results at every angle."[9] There are discussions of key indicators, trends,and expectations affecting organization libraries and a review of related studies undertaken since 1980 to support the conceptual framework. A significant core of the data is provided by discussions on the usage and effectiveness of special library services, the role of the library providing access to information in documents, the use and effectiveness of automated database search services and current awareness services along with a discussion of the functions performed by and services provided by special libraries. Quantification of those products and services is the fabric of this work. Productivity measures are given by the authors, as are unit costs of services. The last chapter of the work reaches the heart of the matter in the discussion of the value and worth of special libraries. The work by Griffiths and King is rich with ideas, models, and concepts to provide approaches to a most elusive issue.

In fact, one of the purposes of Griffiths and King's closing chapter is to show that the "value derived is generally substantially greater than the price paid for information and information services."[10] In following the data presented in the book and the analysis of those data, the conclusion drawn—"It seems abundantly clear that library services pay for themselves by orders of magnitude"[11]—is not only logical but clearly derived from the data presented. Once again, the Special Libraries Association research program has provided a vehicle through the research grant to approach one of the most significant questions to the profession. This study, as well as the others outlined in this chapter, clearly raises issues in terms of what information professionals need to know to do their jobs more effectively.

A research grant has also been awarded by the Special Libraries Association for 1993. Marilyn White will serve as the principal investigator in a study entitled "Measuring Customer Satisfaction and Quality of Service in Special Libraries." As stated in the grant proposal,

> The primary outcome ... is the development of an instrument for measuring
> customer satisfaction which can be used, together with a model of service
> quality, to measure the quality of services in special libraries. The research
> is not limited to a particular kind of library so the instrument will be
> applicable in several kinds of special libraries.[12]

Aside from the growing core of major research efforts funded by SLA research grants, there has been a continuation of other research efforts. For example, Forest Woody Horton Jr. has recently completed his research on emerging jobs and positions for information professionals. The results of this work have been published as Occasional Paper Number Four in the SLA Occasional Paper Series under the title *Extending the Librarian's Domain: A Survey of Emerging Occupation Opportunities for Librarians and Information Professionals*.

In addition, the Special Libraries Association will provide a monetary contribution to the Fédération Internationale de Documentation) (FID) to assist in the funding of a study of the knowledge, competencies, and skills required by the modern information professional. The study, "Survey of the Modern Information Professional", will be conducted by Molly Wolfe. SLA will play a role in the project by providing input, comments, and insights into the various phases of the project.

Another very practical research effort has been the development of a brief piece on multimedia. The purpose is to provide an introduction to the new media environment through the exploration of multimedia technologies in relationship to the special libraries community. The work covers the basics from defining multimedia to forms of multimedia as well as its planning, design, and management. Closing the work are specific examples of multimedia applications in special library settings to bring the conceptual to the practical level. The results of this work are available as the SLA information kit *An Introduction to the Issues and Applications of Interactive Multimedia for Information Specialists* by Nicholas Givotovsky.

In summary, there is a multifaceted approach to the research efforts supported and put forth by the Special Libraries Association. As has been described, the research is intended to provide data, methodologies, and input to the core issues within the information profession. Issues such as value, emerging opportunities, and new technologies are not at all peripheral to information professionals' jobs, but rather approach their very essence. The research supported by the Special Libraries Association does in fact hold the key to the future by addressing performance issues. Indeed, the value issue has been regarded as vital for some time and will only become more vital in this continuously changing economic and information environment. From small to large-scale studies, it is important to support this type of work and relate the results to the working environment. The research results and their use create a kind of symbiotic relationship with the information professional—one which cannot be ignored and one in which all information professionals should share.

Figure 1
SLA Research Agenda

1.0 *Futures*
1.1 What is the impact of the projections of futurists (as identified in the literature) on the special library?
1.2 What technologies currently in the development stage will impact special libraries? How will impact these technologies impact?

2.0 *Current/User Issues*
2.1 How do people decide what they need to know? How do they learn or find what they need to know?
2.2 How can artificial intelligence applications and expert systems facilitate access to source and content information?
2.3 How will AI applications and expert systems change user access and interaction with computerized databases?
2.4 What are information seeking and using behaviors of people in different professions or fields of work?
2.5 What are the design considerations for question-answering or fact-providing online systems?
2.6 What consumer behavior models can be adapted for use by librarians?

3.0 *Measures of Productivity and Value*
3.1 What are existing measures of productivity and value resulting from information access and use? How can these measures be used by special libraries?
3.2 How do clients/users value information?
3.3 To what extent is there a difference between the cost of information and its perceived value?
3.4 What is the relationship between library/information services and corporate or institutional success?
3.5 How can existing cost/benefit methodologies be used by the special librarian?

4.0 *Client/User Satisfaction Measures*
4.1 How can existing consumer satisfaction measurement methods be adapted to the needs of special libraries? What additional measures are needed?
4.2 What is the role of client/user expectations in measuring quality and value of service?
4.3 What are client/user perceptions about the quality of information services?
4.4 What techniques can be used to measure the potential value of new services?
4.5 What can librarians learn from other service businesses, e.g., airlines, hotels, hospitals?
4.6 What corporate marketing strategies can be adapted to marketing the services of special libraries?

5.0 *Staffing*

5.1 What measures and methods are available to assess optimum staff size and organizational structures in special libraries?

5.2 What data and criteria are needed to optimize library staffing?

June 1989

References

1. Drake, Miriam A. "Research and Special Libraries," *Special Libraries* 80(4): Fall 1989, pp. 264-68.
2. *President's Task Force on the Value of the Information Professional.* Final Report for the 78th Annual Conference in Anaheim, California. June 1987, p. 9.
3. Ibid., p. 10.
4. Matarazzo, James M., Laurence Prusak, and Michael R. Gauthier. *Valuing Corporate Libraries: A Survey of Senior Managers.* Washington, D.C.: SLA and Temple, Barker & Sloane, 1990.
5. Prusak, Laurence and James M. Matarazzo. *Information Management and Japanese Success.* Washington, D.C.: SLA, 1992.
6. Marshall, Joanne G. *The Impact of the Special Library on Corporate Decision-Making.* Washington, D.C.: SLA, 1993.
7. Griffiths, José-Marie and Donald King. *Special Libraries: Increasing the Information Edge.* Washington, D.C.: SLA, 1993, p 1.
8. Ibid., pp. 8-9.
9. Ibid., p. 3.
10. Ibid., p. 173.
11. Ibid., p. 190.
12. White, Marilyn. From the grant proposal "Measuring Customer Satisfaction and Quality of Service in Special Libraries." Grant in progress funded by SLA. 1993.

Chapter 10
Records Management
and the Corporate Library
Candy Schwartz

An organization seeking to make decisions for current action and future direction needs knowledge of its own internal strengths and weaknesses, and of the forces influencing its relationships with the external world. Much of this knowledge is gathered from two sources within the organization: the library and records management. Librarians are charged with selecting and packaging information from principally external sources, whereas records managers oversee the corporate memory reflected in internally generated sources.

Records management, as an organizational unit that provides an information-based service, competes with library services for attention and for resources. Both are cost centers, and the cost benefits of both are often difficult to substantiate in any direct manner. In organizations that have a records management program as well as a library, the managers of each must understand the articulation between the roles and responsibilities of the two. In organizations with no records management program, library managers would be well advised (and are best qualified) to consider taking up this responsibility. This chapter provides a basic understanding of records management as a set of activities and as a profession currently seeking new definitions and directions.

A Brief Historical Note

Some of the earliest recordings of humankind are known to be business information (census records, territorial demarcations, tax rosters), so in a sense records management has been part of managing communities and organizations since such social structures began. The need to manage business records was a significant influence on, and was in turn exacerbated by, all of the same developments that have influenced the history of librarianship: writing, papermaking, printing, reproduction, and data processing. Just as developments in information retrieval were necessitated by the information explosion of the 1940s and 1950s, modern records management finds its roots in the paperwork inefficiencies experienced by governments in the same era, and in the recommendations for improved record-keeping procedures made by those governments.[1]

Implementing Records Management

Records management is "the application of systematic and scientific control to all of the recorded information that an organization needs to do business."[2] This is a sweeping responsibility, taken in its broadest sense. The strict interpretation of "recorded information" for the records manager is usually taken to mean *internally created* recorded information (e.g., personnel records, correspondence files, policies, directives, financial records, and so on), in whatever format and on whatever medium.

The principal activities of records management are directed to that systematic control. The basic steps of a records management program from start to finish are as follows.

- Records selection and inventory. This involves discovering what recorded information an organization possesses, and registering for each record *series* (collection of similar items) its title, location, contents, format, quantity, condition, arrangement, storage, provenance, destination, and role. In a large and venerable organization this is likely to be the most time-consuming part of a newly instituted records management program. It is also one of the more sensitive, involving physical invasion of territory, including file cabinets and computer disks.
- Records retention and disposition. Once the inventory is completed, decisions are then made as to how long to keep a record series, in what format(s), and how to dispose of it. Records are appraised for different values, usually expressed in units of time. These include *administrative value* in helping the company do business; *legal value* in ensuring that the company meets its legal rights and obligations, including the record-keeping requirements of local, regional, and national authorities; *fiscal value*; *research or scientific value*; and *archival or historical value*, considering the needs of the organization and of social historians. A final *retention value* is then negotiated with the approval of legal, fiscal, and administrative departments. A *retention schedule* records these decisions and includes details about how long records will remain active (occupying expensive office space and cabinetry), how long they will remain inactive (maintained in a records center in more compact storage), and whether and how they will be destroyed or permanently retained.

  Records retention and disposition constitute an area where records managers bear a great deal of responsibility and accountability. For one thing, maintaining unnecessary records is very expensive in terms of space, and makes it more difficult to retrieve what is really needed. An equally important point is that retention decisions have a direct impact on the results of litigation, when an organization's records may be open to inspection. Records managers must be thoroughly up-to-date about the retention recommendations set forth in federal and local statutes. Further, they must ensure that the retention decisions they make are actually carried through by departmental record-series owners. The records management literature is replete with examples of the disastrous consequences of poor retention practices.
- Vital records management. Vital records (those which are absolutely necessary for the survival of an organization) are identified during inventory and retention, and special attention is paid to protecting these records. In some cases protection may simply mean ensuring that several copies of the record are dispersed in the normal course of operations. Alternatively, it may mean vaulting, off-site protection, microfilming, and so on. Companies that lose vital records in a disaster are more likely to fail following attempts to start up again.
- Disaster preparedness. Records managers are responsible for assessing risks to records (ranging from natural disaster to theft of a letter), and for instituting plans to minimize the likelihood and results of disaster. This demands expertise in building and space management and security systems, and involves working with local police and fire authorities. Records managers also need to understand the preservation and recovery procedures for all the various media on which information is recorded.

Records Management Activities

Carrying through a records management program involves a number of supportive activities and skills.

- <u>File organization and handling</u>. Records managers have to be thoroughly familiar with a wide range of filing equipment (for all types of media) so that they can make informed decisions about what is cost-efficient *and* most appropriate for use. In addition to well-managed physical storage, another desirable outcome of a records management program is consistent and standardized filing procedures throughout an organization. File maintenance pertains as well to records stored in company or commercial records centers, that is, not in active use in offices. Records center management involves optimizing the use of storage space, and developing retrieval and copying services.

- <u>Forms management</u>. Most internal business information is collected on forms, ranging from letterhead to time cards. Controlling forms creation and inventory offers opportunities to make information gathering, storage, and generation more efficient from the start.

- <u>Reprographics and micrographics</u>. Since duplicating technologies are the largest source of records generation, records managers are well advised to have some control over office copying practices. Records managers are also involved much more frequently in microfilming projects than are librarians, because microfilm is a widely used method of records retention and preservation.

- <u>Database and information technologies.</u> There are several reasons why records managers must be au courant with the latest information technologies. Clearly the information gathered in selection, inventory, and retention lends itself to database management. Even the simplest of database management systems can easily maintain the files needed to manage records, and can generate reports such as retention schedules, vital records schedules, transfer lists (when records are shifted from an office to storage), and so on. Dozens of purpose-designed records management software products are on the market, and many more locally designed systems are in place.

  Additionally, much corporate information is stored in machine-readable form. This means that records managers must understand the special difficulties of inventorying, retaining, and protecting or disposing of electronic records. Hardware and software must be inventoried as well, since changes in either can render a record unreadable.

  Finally, as organizations move toward integrated electronic information management systems, records managers find themselves involved in wide-scale projects involving optical technologies, scanning, imaging, and local-area and wide-area networking.

- <u>General management skills.</u> As heads of units or departments, records managers also engage in the same activities as any manager: planning, budgeting, personnel management, space design, systems analysis, and evaluation of services.

Records Management Training

Clearly records managers share a number of skill sets and knowledge areas with librarians. Both handle information in a wide variety of formats. Both are concerned with acquisition, storage, retrieval, service to users, filing, preservation, and weeding. Both use the same technological tools. The differences have to do with where the information comes from (external versus internal sources), and the nature of the information. Librarians collect information resources because they record knowledge, records managers because they record business operations.

The biggest difference between records managers and librarians has to do with academic preparation, and the related fact that records management is not a recognized scholarly field possessing a body of theory and research. The professional credential for library and information science is widely recognized to be a master's degree from an institution accredited by the American Library Association, and that has been the case for many decades. There is no equivalent in records management. In fact very few institutions in the United States offer even an undergraduate degree in what could be construed as records management,[3] although bachelor's and master's degree programs in many other professional and disciplinary areas incorporate courses in records management and related topics. There is, as Pemberton points out, "no one universally recognized and required educational credential...."[4] The Institute of Certified Records Managers (ICRM) administers a certification program requiring examinations, case studies, and on-the-job experience, but it is not widely recognized by employers. Working records managers may rise through the ranks with little in the way of higher education, or may have advanced degrees in business administration, information systems, computer science, history, or library and information science, among others.

The Professional Community

The principal professional group is the Association of Records Managers and Administrators (ARMA International), with well over 10,000 members. ARMA publishes a large number of industry guidelines and other monographs and the journal Records Management Quarterly, and holds one large conference each year. Other groups with a records management affiliation include Aslib, Association for Federal Information Resources Management (AFFIRM), Association for Information and Image Management (AIIM), Association for Information Management (AIM), Information Industry Association (IIA), International Information Management Congress (IMC), National Association of Government Archives and Records Administrators (NAGARA), and Society for Information Management (SIM). There are also specialized groups in many professional and industrial sectors (for instance, the American Health Information Management Association).

As might be expected in a field with an ill-defined academic standing, the professional journal literature (see the Appendix) is largely practical in nature, and access to it is scattered through a large number of indexing services, of which the most productive are Inspec, *ABI/Inform*, and *Library and Information Science Abstracts*.[5] Tables of contents listing services such as CARL UnCover can also be useful sources. As a group, records managers are more likely to scan current journals in the field, rather than to do research in secondary services. To this point few records managers would appear to make use of the Internet, and there is no records management LISTSERV list. Personal networking and continuing education needs are largely served by local chapters of ARMA.

Records Managers and Corporate Librarians

Living through the same fiscal upheavals as corporate librarians, records managers are grappling with the same problems, and are emerging with remarkably similar thoughts and strategies. Seeking to enhance their perceived value, records managers have begun to redefine their field and their mission. Titles such as "information resources manager," or "information and records manager" reflect a shift in emphasis, as do the current texts prepared by, for instance, Penn, Morddel, Pennix, and Smith[6]; Ricks and Gow[7]; and Wallace, Lee, and Schubert[8]). The themes of information resources management (IRM) are that

- information is an asset, on a par with other resources (capital, materials, personnel), with attendant costs and benefits;
- information has an identifiable life cycle within an organization, from creation through dissemination and use to retirement; and
- information should be managed in a systematic and scientific manner.

The practice of information resources management (as expressed in Horton's classic work[9]) entails a delineation of information resources (including external and internal sources, services and systems), followed by an analysis of the requirements of individuals and departments for those resources. The result is a profile of who uses what resources throughout the organization. This affords a systematic and detailed assessment of costs and benefits, and a basis for streamlining, strategic planning, introducing uniform and consistent practices, charging back or making budgetary allocations for information activities, and generally managing information resources in the most effective and efficient way.

The practice of information resources management extends the records management sphere of influence to a point where it converges upon that of the corporate library. Two quotations from the recent records management literature express an aspiration which is common to both groups.

> The intent of this approach is to manage information as a corporate resource rather than a strictly departmental or functional resource. This approach attempts to remove the artificial boundaries between information resources, whether by reason of media, location, or departmental "ownership," in order to create a single, integrated information environment so that information becomes another resource which supports the goals of the organization, as opposed to working against those goals.[10]
>
> ...our strength is in how much money information management can EARN for the organization, and how we as records managers can contribute to corporate success by ensuring that only information that is NEEDED is produced or received and only THAT information is maintained and kept accessible.[11]

How similar this is to what we hear from Prusak and Matarazzo,[12] Eddison[13] or Svoboda,[14] among others, in the literature of corporate librarianship. From sources on both sides we also hear of the need to enhance perceived value, target markets for services, be more attuned to user needs, and understand the corporate structure (and how to manipulate it). Both groups are receiving the same message.

In some cases that message is accompanied by a call for alliance, both educationally[15] and functionally.[16] An educational alliance is attractive to both parties. Library and information science programs would benefit in enrolment and in involvement with a new professional partner. A fully accredited and well-established higher degree could allow records managers to be more competitive with peer managers possessing master's degrees in business administration, computer science, and the like. More to the point, the curricular content of library and information science already embraces much of what records managers need: management, evaluation, systems analysis, user services, indexing, information technologies, archives, preservation, and so on. More than a third of the nation's ALA-accredited schools of library and information science already offer records management coursework.[17] Another advantage to an educational alliance is that records management would then have access to a body of theory and research which relates to information seeking, information use, user behavior, and related topics. (See, for instance, Goodman.[18])

Functional alliance is more difficult to achieve, especially in an existing organization. It is one thing to maintain that all information units should work together for the greater good of the organization, and quite another to bring that result about. If both records managers and librarians are being called upon in their respective professions to become true information resources managers, several scenarios could play themselves out in any given situation. Both units could work together voluntarily and effectively. Either unit could merge with or subsume the other. Both could be merged with or subsumed by a parallel unit (say, for instance, management information systems). Both could find themselves reporting to a new intermediate-level manager. In all but the first scenario, one or more units stand to lose resources and/or status.

In time, educational alliances may pave the way for the functional alliances. In the meantime, it would certainly not be in any company's best interests for librarians and records managers (and other managers) to be pitted against each other in turf wars. Corporate librarians who enhance their talent base with a knowledge of records management will gain a richer understanding of the complex information structures of organizations. In the absence of records management programs, they can provide a service with clear added values of promoting efficiency and cost savings. In the long run, they will be in the best position to move into leadership roles in developing or contributing to integrated information resources management systems.

References

1. Schwartz, Candy, and Peter Hernon. *Records Management and the Library*. New York: Ablex, 1993. Chapter Two: "Historical Background."

2. Robek, Mary E., Gerald F. Brown, and Wilmer O. Maedke. *Information and Records Management* 3rd ed. Encino, Calif.: Glencoe, 1987 p. 5.

3. Association of Records Managers and Administrators. *Directory of Collegiate Schools Offering Courses & Majors in Records & Information Management*. Prairie Village, Kans.: ARMA International, 1993.

4. Pemberton, J. Michael. "Education for Records Managers: Rigor Mortis or New Directions?" *Records Management Quarterly* 25 (3) July 1991, pp. 50-54

5. Schwartz and Hernon, op. cit., pp. 14-15.

6. Penn, Ira A., Anne Morddel, Gail Pennix, and Kelvin Smith. *Records Management Handbook*. Brookfield, Vt.: Gower, 1989.

7. Ricks, Betty R., and Kay F. Gow. *Information Resource Management: A Records Systems Approach*, 2nd ed. Cincinnati, Ohio: South-Western Publishing, 1988.

8. Wallace, Patricia E., JoAnn Lee, and Dexter R. Schubert. *Records Management: Integrated Information Systems*, 3rd ed. Englewood Cliffs, N.J.: Prentice-Hall, 1992.

9. Horton, F.W., Jr. *Information Resources Management*. Englewood Cliffs, N.J.: Prentice-Hall, 1985.

10. Attinger, Monique L. "Integrated Information Management: A Real World Theory," *Records Management Quarterly* 27 (3), July 1993, pp. 12-16.

11. Summerville, John R. "Records Management: A 'Now' Kinda Thing?" *Records Management Quarterly* 26 (1) January 1992 pp. 10-13.

12. Prusak, Laurence, and James M. Matarazzo. "Tactics for Corporate Library Success," *Library Journal*, 115 (15) September 15, 1990 pp. 45-46.

13. Eddison, Betty. "Strategies for Success (Or Opportunities Galore)," *Special Libraries*, 81 (2) Spring 1990 pp. 111-18.

14. Svoboda, Olga. "The Special Library as a Competitive Intelligence Center," *Electronic Library* 9 (4/5) August-October 1991 pp. 239-44.

15. Pemberton, op. cit.

16. Wright, Craig. "Corporate Records Management and the Librarian," *Special Libraries* 82 (4) Fall 1991 pp. 300-304.

17. Association of Records Managers and Administrators, op. cit.

18. Goodman, Susan K. "Information Needs for Management Decision-Making," *Records Management Quarterly*, 27 (4) October 1993 pp. 12-23.

Appendix: Journals in Records Management

<u>Core Journals</u>

IMC Journal

Inform

International Journal of Information Management

Recordfacts Update

Records and Retrieval Report

Records Management Journal (ceased publication in 1993)

Records Management Quarterly

<u>Principal Peripheral Journals</u>

American Archivist

Archives

Archives & Museum Informatics

Aslib Information

Bulletin of the American Society for Information Science

Datamation

Document Image Automation

Government Computer News

Information Processing and Management

Information Systems

Information Systems Management

Information Week

International Journal of Micrographics & Optical Technology

Journal of Management Information Systems

Journal of Systems Management

Microcomputers for Information Management

MIS Quarterly

The Office

Chapter 11
Total Quality Management:
How to Improve Your Library
Without Losing Your Mind
Barbara M. Spiegelman

Your library or information center is under the gun. Costs are too high, productivity is too low, and the dreaded phrases "overhead," "cost center," "reduced staff," or "budget cuts" are being bandied about by your management or administration.

You need to examine the efficiency of your processes today and identify the improvements you will put into place tomorrow and beyond. If you do not have a Total Quality initiative in place, you are probably caught in the soft data/hard data dilemma that surrounds knowledge workers: "I know we do valuable work and do it well — I just can't prove it." The techniques of Total Quality Management can help you to improve both the reality and the perception of your library service in a way that will satisfy even the most statistically minded manager with data that illustrate your point. It does not matter whether you call it Total Quality Management (TQM), Continuous Quality Improvement (CQI), or Continuous Process Improvement (CPI); the journey to improvement by any name can get you where you want to go.

What TQM Can — and Cannot — Do

It is a common error to assume that TQM techniques are guarantees — of safety, of stability, of security. TQM *does not guarantee* that your library will be safe from all harm. It is likely that your organization and mine will continue to be affected by upturns or downturns in the business cycle, resource shortages, and competing priorities. It *does not guarantee* that your library will not have to make constant adjustments to changes in a larger organization. And lastly, all of your dedicated efforts at TQM *do not guarantee* that your job will be forever secure. It is possible to have high TQM results and still be in a bad situation. It may have more to do with your corporate climate and environment than anything you are doing. There is no automatic link between profitability and TQM.

What TQM *can do* is to ensure that every effort you make in your information center, every expenditure of time, of people, and of money, is aimed at one goal: customer satisfaction. The outcomes of effective TQM are usually smooth work flow, increased productivity, reduced cycle time, and reduced cost. These are the qualities that create customer satisfaction. Most organizations will support those services that are highly valued by customers. TQM can make your library or information center that service.

There are those who try to make TQM complex. Do not let them do this. TQM is nothing more than an organized approach to improvement. It requires you to *identify* the value of your products and services from your customers' frame of reference, *map* the processes you use to deliver those products and services, *measure* the effectiveness of those improvements, and *communicate* the improved measures to your staff, your customers, and your management. This approach is illustrated in Figure 1.

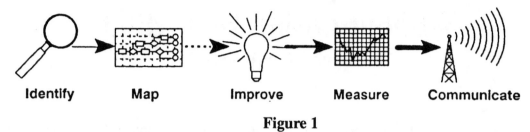

Identify   Map   Improve   Measure   Communicate

Figure 1

When your TQM process is more advanced, you can insert one more step: benchmarking, or finding out how others accomplish the same tasks, and choosing the best practices to reach your own goals.

This chapter does not chronicle the history and growth of the TQM initiative in the United States. It focuses on the application of the steps listed in Figure 1 to libraries and information centers, particularly those beginning the TQM process. The discussion includes methods for starting the journey, identifying perils and pitfalls to avoid along the way, and making some recommendations on how to keep your head when those around you are losing theirs.

The Briefest of Backgrounds

In the 1950s and 1960s, it was hard for a business or profession in the United States not to do well. A growing economy, the constant improvement of technology, and an ever-more-educated work force promised to go on forever. At that time, we laughed about products that came out of the Far East. The phrase "Made in Japan" on an article almost guaranteed that it would fall apart within 24 hours.

In the 1970's and early 1980's, our laughter stopped. We began to see a decline in the quality of American goods, while the cost of the goods increased. Our market share of many items began to decrease. Americans were not willing to pay more money for lower quality — and neither was anyone else.

During the same period, the quality of Japanese products improved significantly. Advanced management methods and economic factors were partially responsible for this improvement. But an equally important factor was their ability to emphasize and successfully embed the concept of *kaizen*, or continuous improvement, into their homogeneous culture. It was the adaptation of *kaizen* to the American idiom that has become the TQM initiative of today. This transfer of idea, ethic, and technique is detailed in hundreds of books, and particularly in the works of Deming and Juran. Read these authors' works for a greater understanding of the theory of TQM, and for wonderful "war stories" about early application of the techniques in American manufacturing plants.

The Big Picture: Planning Your Journey

There are as many approaches, methodologies, and graphics illustrating TQM as there are corporations in America. If your organization has a TQM approach in place, you should concentrate on fitting your information center improvement initiative into that approach. You will be able to speak to others in your organization with a common vocabulary, share experiences, successes, and near misses within a common framework, and be able to compare your progress to that of others on a common scale.

If your organization has no TQM approach in place, you may want to check with others in your industry or field to see what has worked comfortably for them. You can also borrow the following approach, taking care to adapt it to your culture.

Within Westinghouse Electric Corporation, we base our TQM initiative around a simple triangle of four imperatives, as shown in Figure 2. Note that the triangle is based on the imperative of management leadership — because those at the top of an organization must set the climate in which TQM can flourish. The apex of the triangle is customer orientation — because that is where all TQM must lead, and where it is ultimately judged.

The four imperatives, or building blocks of TQM, are divided into twelve criteria, and each of these is divided into subcriteria. The subcriteria (49 in all) are the mortar (or nitty-gritty) of the building blocks. As any organization within Westinghouse begins the journey to continuous improvement, they ask themselves questions based on these same 49 subcriteria. A beginning set of questions for libraries and information centers based on these subcriteria is listed in "Total Quality Management in Libraries: Getting Down to the Real Nitty-Gritty.

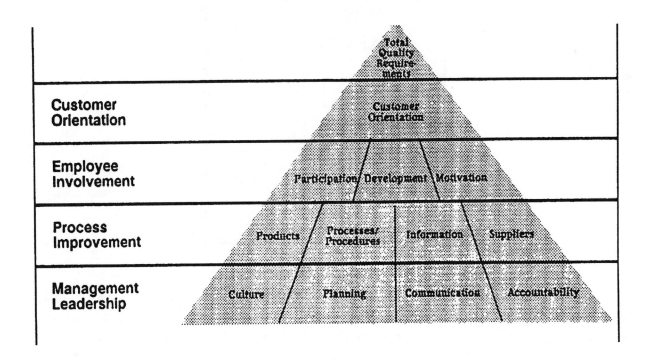

Figure 2
"Getting Down to the Real Nitty-Gritty."[1]

The Journey Begins

It is time to start your journey. Apply the following steps to your information center. Take them one at a time and at your own pace.

Identify

- What do we do? (What is our mission? What are our products and services?)
- Are we doing the right things? (Which of our products and services do we think are of value to the organization?)
- How well do we do them? (Which of our products and services do our customers value?)

Begin with a staff brainstorming session. List all the products and services that your information center offers. Include everything from the standard library services that come immediately to mind (building the collection, cataloging, loaning materials, reference, and research) to those things you do almost without thinking (directing queries to the most appropriate person within the organization, posting the corporation's quarterly report on bulletin boards, alerting customers of upcoming subscription increases so they can budget accordingly). Once your list of products and services is complete, divide them into broad categories. Figure 3 provides a sample list of categories to get you started.

Library/Info Center Services
Circulation
Current awareness
Database design
Document delivery
Information analysis
Literature searching
Ready reference
Subscription management

Figure 3

You and your staff must now rank the categories two ways: first in order of your perception of their value to the organization (A for most valuable, B for next valuable, and so on), and then based on your perception of how well you perform the service on a scale of 1 to 5 (5 is the best possible rating). The value rating must be a *forced ranking,* that is, there can be only one A, one B, one C, and so forth. Using this method, you force yourself and your staff to begin weighing products and services against one another. I have found it useful to do my ranking separately from the staff, and then to discuss our varying perceptions.

Seeing Through Your Customers' Eyes

The object of the TQM journey is satisfaction and continuous improvement from the customer's frame of reference. Remember that phrase, "from the customer's frame of reference." It is one of the most important concepts within TQM. It is easy to find yourself redesigning processes, retraining people, and in general turning your world upside down to improve a process you consider important. But if that improvement is of little value to the customer, your journey has taken a dangerous detour.

To make sure your efforts will be of value to the customer, present the same list of product and service categories to your customers for their ranking. You can do this through mail surveys, focus groups, short presentations at group meetings, or by questioning customers when they are in the library. Beware of limiting your data gathering to only those who currently use your services. Good customers will have valuable input — but so will noncustomers. They can tell you what information they need that you do not supply, what additional services would be valuable to them, and — very important — where they are getting that information and those services now. This is a quick way to identify your competition.

A simple way to gather value and performance data is to have your customers rank your products/ services according to the same ranking process used by your staff. First, have the customer perform a forced ranking of the value of your products or services (A for most valuable, B for next most valuable, etc.). Then, have the customer rate how well you perform each service. Table 1 gives an example of this method.

Product/Service	Value (A, B, C, etc.)	Performance (1 to 5)
Circulation		
Current awareness		
Database design		
Document delivery		
Information analysis		
Literature searching		
Ready reference		
Subscription management		

Table 1

Once you have collected all the data from your staff and customers, you must compare the results. Table 2 provides an example which shows the differing perceptions that exist.

Products and Services	Staff Value Ranking	Customer Value Ranking	Staff Performance Ranking	Customer Performance Ranking
Circulation	B	F	2	4
Current awareness	C	C	3	3
Database design	D	D	5	5
Document delivery	A	E	5	5
Information analysis	F	A	3	2
Literature searching	E	B	4	3
Ready reference	G	H	4	4
Subscription management	H	G	4	4

Table 2

This example shows you how easy it is to get off the track of TQ. Everyone seems to be in agreement that the staff of this hypothetical library do an excellent job at document delivery. The trouble is, the staff think document delivery are very valuable, and the customers do not value it much at all! The staff is not satisfied with their circulation performance. Left to their own devices, they might spend a significant amount of time investigating and implementing a new circulation system. The customers, however, are pleased with circulation and wish the staff would spend available time and money on developing literature search and information analysis methodologies and improving their current awareness service. Applying TQM principles has helped identify clear priorities. This library now knows where to put its resources to improve customer satisfaction.

Map

Before you can improve a process, you must be able to answer this question:

• How do we do it today? (*What are the steps of the current process?*)

The best way we have found to map processes is to use "stickies", those lifesaving stick-on note originally invented by the 3M Corporation. We use one color of "stickies" to map the current process, and a different color to map an improved process. The "stickies" are ideal mapping tools because they can be moved around with ease. We have done this mapping both formally and informally, using a team facilitator the first time, and the next time standing around a counter with everyone moving their own "stickies" as needed.

The important thing is to put in order the exact steps of the process the way it is done today. Once you are sure you have captured all of the steps, mark the time it takes for completion of each step on its "stickie". Total the times of all the steps to find the current cycle time for the entire process. (Do not forget to add in any time you must wait for others between steps.) Translate that time into a cost. If a process takes a total of five days in your shop, divided between two people, use their hourly cost to give you a ballpark figure. Five-decimal-point calculations are not needed here. You want to know *approximately* what this process is costing you now.

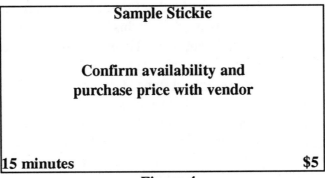

Figure 4

Do not stop here. Each of the processes you just identified is probably made up of subprocesses. You should now map each of the major subprocesses. For example, if you are trying to improve document delivery, you may have subprocesses to identify the appropriate document, identify a source, place the order, check in the material, distribute the material to the customer, and charge for your services. When you reach the critical stage of identifying measures, you will find these sub-process maps very useful.

Improve

There are a myriad of questions you can ask yourself and your staff to begin seeing the process in a new way.

- Why do we do this step to begin with?
- Are we repeating (entering data/rewriting/recalculating) something the customer or another department has already done?
- If so, can this step be eliminated or pared down?
- Does the process flow well, without backtracking to the same people?
- Are there obvious bottlenecks, caused by wait time, competing deadlines, etc?
- Is there significant "dead time," that is, time when nothing is happening? If so, can two tasks be handled concurrently?
- Are we doing something manually we could automate?
- Are we creating three spreadsheets (one for orders, one for subscriptions, one for statistics) that could be combined into one?
- Are there too many handoffs in a process? If five people are getting involved (sometimes twice!), you have a place to begin streamlining.
- Are the right people doing each task?

Prepare yourself for defensiveness. The kinds of questions you are asking here can be very threatening. When you ask "Do we really need to do this?" the people who currently do that task already see themselves in the unemployment line. Their natural response is to think of several solid-gold reasons why you must continue the task. It takes perseverance and a calm demeanor to overcome these barriers. One way is to point out some of the other tasks these people might be able to accomplish if you could eliminate the one in question.

It is very valuable to have several customers involved in this process. They not only have an outsider's view (that keeps asking "why"), but can also bring you ideas or solutions that have worked in their own groups. A process improvement that piggybacks onto something someone else has already tested shortens the improvement learning curve.

Now it is time to improve the process. Using the insights you acquired during analysis of the current process and a second color of "stickie", start playing with the steps of the process, and moving the steps around. Once you have mapped the improved process, it is always a good idea to go back and compare the new map with the old — to make sure no steps have been forgotten.

This simplified method is not meant to imply that improvement is easy — or that you will complete this process in fifteen minutes. But in most cases, identifying potential improvements is not brain surgery. Most of our processes got where they are because we designed them quickly to meet a need, jury-rigged something to fill in until we got something better (and never did), or became outdated because we never reviewed them. You will probably see improvements so quickly that you will be asking why you have been doing it this way for so long.

Measure

Choosing the final aspect(s) of the process to improve and what to measure is a matter of identifying what is most important to your organization. Once you have identified the improvements that need to be made, you are ready to answer the following questions.

- What is the current baseline? (*How good/fast/accurate are we now?*)
- What is our goal? (*How good /fast/accurate would we like to be when we have improved the process?*)
- How will we know when we get there? (*What do we need to monitor, and how often?*)

Measures are tough. It is not unusual to identify and track several measures (or more!) — only to find that they do not really tell you what you want to know. Do not be disheartened by these false starts. At the beginning of your journey you will learn as much from the process of TQM — identifying value-added services, establishing baselines, streamlining processes, initiating change, and measuring progress — as you will from final numbers.

The best way we have found to identify appropriate measures is, again, to brainstorm. Make sure you have your *improved* process and subprocess maps close at hand. Begin by labeling three flip charts *cycle time, cost improvement,* and *customer satisfaction.* (Yes, this is very simplistic. It also works.) Begin by listing all the possible things you could measure about the improved processes and subprocesses. For example, if part of the subprocess of document delivery is "place order with vendor," some possible measures are "time from customer request until order is placed with vendor," "time from customer request until cost of order is known," "time from order to delivery," and "cost for rush delivery versus normal delivery." These measures fit into either the cycle-time reduction or the cost-reduction measurement categories.

If you are in the middle of a tremendous budget crunch, opt for improvements that cut costs. Measure the cost-savings of delivering the service using the improved process. If your organization is more focused on increasing productivity, opt for improvements that reduce cycle time. All improvements are valuable, but in every organization, some are more valuable than others. Know your organization, and choose accordingly.

A word of caution — In any session in which you are trying to zero in on measures, you will probably find that people keep trying to come back to "counting." We have all become excellent at quantitative measures: x literature searches completed; y reference questions answered; z materials circulated. These measures do indeed indicate that we are not just sitting around the information center twiddling our thumbs; we are serving customers per their request. But the numbers themselves do not tell the whole story. We could potentially serve one million customers — and all of them poorly! Now we must develop the same expertise at qualitative measures. *How well are we serving those customers? Are we providing the services at the most appropriate cost? Is our process as efficient as it could be?* Developing the "qualitative" mind-set takes time. It may be worth the time to have your group expand the following list:

Quantitative	**Qualitative**
Cycle time	Customer satisfaction
- time to shelf	- valuation of services
Cost reduction	Effectiveness of marketing
- cost of literature searches	- % of collection borrowed

Don't wrench away the counting measures — for now, take satisfaction in moving them to the back seat.

Less Is More

I believe that you are better off with a few measures you can track easily than a whole raft of them. I know of organizations that are measuring thirty items. Their bulletin boards are so littered with graphs you can't identify a trend to save your soul. In our technical library, for the past two years we have monitored the quality and accuracy of literature searches, turnaround time (meeting customer deadlines), and overall customer satisfaction. We have always been good at meeting customer deadlines. In the summer of this year, we had three straight months of meeting 100 percent of customer deadlines *without renegotiating any of those deadlines with the customer.* And some of those deadlines were a half hour or less. When we made those numbers, we knew it — and we made sure everyone else did too.

Once the measures are decided, you need to find a reasonable way to collect the data and monitor the measure. The ideal is to have the measure built into an automated system — for example, to send customers a survey with every SDI you deliver via their e-mail address. The e-mail includes a reply form which the customer must complete before they can exit the e-mail system. The replies are gathered in one e-mail ID, and mapped to a spreadsheet. Welcome to paradise.

Most of us do not live in paradise. You can gather the same data through paper surveys, spot phone calls, etc. The key is to have an internal process that does not burden the staff. We gather all customer surveys in one area and one person analyzes them and reports statistics. She passes these to the person who charts our progress and hangs the final graph. I report the year-to-date progress on goals in my monthly report to my manager. And most important, the complete pile of surveys (written in the customers' own hands) is routed to the complete staff. Data are gathered, monitored, and communicated with a minimum of effort.

Remember the basic goal of measurement: to track improvement. If you were able to complete your process maps with any degree of accuracy, you know your baseline and are ready to begin tracking improvement. If your process maps did not provide a baseline, you may need to monitor your current performance for a while. If you can backfill any of these data from statistics you have kept or past surveys, you may only need to measure the current process for a month or two. If you are starting fresh, you should monitor your current process for at least three months, or long enough to eliminate any of those weird events that skew the measure. For example, if your customers get new budgets in January, you probably see an upswing in demand for literature searches that month. Significantly increased demand may make your performance against your goal decline. In the dog days of August, when no one is requesting research, your performance will look sterling. To really analyze trends, you need to have enough data.

And now we come to the fun part.

Communicate

Communication brings your quality journey full circle. It allows you to tell everyone — your management, your staff, your colleagues, and yourself — where you have been, where you want to go, how you will get there, and how the trip is progressing.

The key to communicating TQM is redundancy and simplicity. Redundancy means that you tell your story often, in many ways, to many levels. For example, you share your progress with your management at least every month. You present statistics and graphs in your monthly report, your quarterly status report, and your year-end report. You mention your continuing progress in presentations to management, administrators, and customers. You communicate progress to your customers through bulletin boards, information center newsletters, on the opening screen of your LAN or e-mail system, and somewhere on your research summaries.

What should the visual communications look like? It is not necessary to overwhelm people with complicated charts. I believe in bar charts and line graphs for dummies: charts whose messages are instantly clear to the viewer. Most of us do not have a degree in statistics. And while the odd manager may enjoy winding his or her way through a regression analysis or falling brick chart, most of us would prefer to see a chart with a line marked goal and a bar that almost reaches it. For trends, we like to see a solid line named 1993 and a dotted line marked 1994 marching across a chart which has a level marked *goal*. These kinds of visuals are not only easier to read and interpret — they are also usually easier to create.

You must communicate all the data (whether good or bad) to your staff. Communication to management and customers will get you visibility, credit, and support. Communications to the people who actually do the work will get you involvement. And once your staff are truly involved in the TQM process, the journey is a pleasure.

Perils and Pitfalls

If you are anything like me, you start your vacation by looking at maps, to see where there may be problems enroute to my destination. Here is my "map" of perils and pitfalls enroute to TQM.

- *Watch out for egos — your own and others.* By definition, the journey to continuous improvement means you must accept that you and your organization are not perfect. We all know this with our heads, but it is hard to accept with our hearts. Try to distance yourself from the process enough so that you do not respond defensively to any ideas for improvement. And as if it is not enough to keep yourself from being defensive, you must keep your staff from feeling that way.

- *Beware of people's reaction to perceived blame.* Present the whole concept of Total Quality with great care. Even the name works against you. When you tell your staff that you want them to produce quality work, their only response can be, "What do you think I have been trying to do all these years?" You must introduce the need for improved quality or productivity in a way that does not blame anyone for past behavior. Concentrate on communicating those things that have changed in your environment. Is money tighter? Is headcount a bigger issue than before — leading to the need for everyone to work more productively to succeed in this new environment? Has the research area or industry changed dramatically, so that the old ways of keeping up with information are now inadequate? Blame anything for the needed changes — except your people.

- *Detour around cynics.* The world is full of them, and the TQM world in particular seems to have a population of cynics that could rival the population of the People's Republic of China. If you let these people get to you, with their messages that "nothing will ever change," or "it's just another way to get rid of headcount," you will be fighting depression most of the time. The only way I have found to personally combat this negative army is to look very closely at the people who are saying these things. Are they people I would normally use as role models? Are they spectacularly successful at what they do? Are they known more for achieving results or for whining? Once I have figured out that they are not who I want to be — I avoid them like the plague. This is not very friendly or very nice behavior on my part, but it is a matter of mental survival.

- *Caution — no closure in sight.* For those of us who are accustomed to bringing everything to some sort of closure or resolution, TQM is difficult. We know that we are not looking for a quick fix. But we figure that somewhere down the line there will come a day, a date, a point, where we can say "I've finished that job." The basic underpinning of *kaizen* is that improvement is continuous. Our journey is not long, it is forever. And on a bad day, forever looks even longer than that. To get over this particular road hazard, I recommend frequent rest stops. Look back often to where you started. Take the time to tell staff members that you could not have made it this far without them — because you could not. Compare your group to others in the organization who are still trying to justify their existence. Write an article about your success for a professional publication. Schedule time with your boss for the express purpose of discussing recent process improvements. Your trip will be no shorter, but it may be a lot more pleasant.

Sanity Check

The time may come when you and your staff feel that TQM is driving you slowly out of your mind. You are trying to serve customers and balance the budget, and TQM seems like another item on everyone's "To Do" list — just what they do not need. Here are some things to keep in mind when those around you are losing theirs.

TQM requires patience. It is not separate from the job — it is the job. As long as you view it as an extra task, it will be a difficult one. Incorporating the mind-set and methods of TQM takes time. Give yourself the time you need. Allow yourself the practice it takes to learn any new tool. Have patience with yourself.

TQM requires involvement. Not just support. Not just words. Not just money. You and every member of your team must be involved in the process, from identifying the services to spreading the word about how far you have come. Do not attempt to lead a TQM effort without being heavily involved yourself. Your people will recognize the "do what I say, not what I do" syndrome.

TQM is more a matter of trends than of today's measure. How are things moving from week to week? from month to month? from one year to the next? Your goal is to get things headed in the right direction and keep them that way. Try to stay focused on the long term.

TQM's best friend is cycle time reduction. It can free people to work on other tasks and can get them away from doing the drudge work that should not be done at all. Improved cycle time usually equals faster service — and faster service equals improved customer satisfaction.

TQM can build teamwork. Teaming your TQM initiative with another department brings multiple dividends. Each department gets the benefit of outside thinking, and the departments build improved products as they improve their ability to work together. This is a win/win situation in anyone's book.

The Endless Journey

Total Quality Management techniques can help library and information center managers to identify, prioritize, and improve processes based on hard data. Techniques for gathering and evaluating customer perceptions are outlined. A roadmap is provided for process improvement. Data on customer perceptions drive the improvement process. Communication techniques to many levels bring the TQM process full circle to begin again. Pitfalls to avoid in the TQM process are outlined.

Like any other journey, TQM requires courage. Courage to leave what is safe, to try new things, to face new challenges, to sometimes fail, and to sometimes feel lost. The road is hazardous, but we are all on the same journey, and there are many who will help you along the way. All you need to do is to pack your suitcase with a few TQM tools and take the first step. I look forward to meeting you along the way.

References

1.   Spiegelman, Barbara M. "Total Quality Management in Libraries: Getting Down to the Real Nitty-Gritty," *Library Management Quarterly* 15 (3) Summer 1992 pp. 12-16.

Techniques recommended in this chapter have been adapted from methods developed by the Westinghouse Productivity and Quality Center. For more information on these methods, contact Carl Arendt, 412/778-5008.

Chapter 12
Effective Information Delivery
Jane L. Rich

The information industry is undergoing a major shift in the way information is distributed to the end user. A 1992 report by Arthur D. Little, Inc., attributes these changes to both customer needs and technology advances. The software products of Lotus Development Corporation have defined and set the standard for desktop computing technology, and Lotus is now leading technological advances in the information industry with its local-area network-based groupware software, Lotus Notes.

Librarians and information specialists are frequently early adopters of information technology because the information industry is driven by technology. At Lotus Development Corporation, the Information Resources Group (IRG) has been on the leading edge of these technology changes. IRG has initiated and explored new electronic information delivery options for its clientele. The fact that Lotus is a major desktop computing player means that electronic delivery is not just an option for end users; it is an imperative. IRG has devoted efforts to electronic information delivery since early days, but the corporate-wide adoption of the network-based information-sharing software, Lotus Notes, allowed IRG to use Lotus Notes as the foundation upon which to build an electronic library that serves the information needs of the entire worldwide Lotus community.

This case study describes the transition of the Lotus Information Resources Group from that of a traditional corporate library based on physical collections and resources to an information resources group focused on promoting electronic access to and delivery of information services through a "virtual" or electronic library. The current IRG mission is to support Lotus's business decision-making process with timely, accurate, accessible, and cost-effective information delivered electronically.

Background

The founders of Lotus Development Corporation supported the development of a centralized information services group right from the beginning of the company (1982). Few information sources were available on the emerging personal computer industry, but the Lotus Library was chartered even before the company issued the first public offering. The library staff endeavored to provide whatever sparse information was available about this new industry to the employees of the corporation. Services provided by IRG consisted of journal and contents routing and a weekly newsletter designed to summarize and highlight industry announcements, events, product introductions, and reviews, and to announce new companies and major players in the industry. A collection of books and trade publications was also established. The library, while available to all staff, delivered information services primarily to the marketing group at Lotus. The Lotus Library was an early adopter of personal computer technology and, in addition to online information retrieval and document delivery, an automated library catalog was among the first electronic information projects begun by the library. The electronic catalog was established using brand-new local-area network software and the only microcomputer-based library automation package on the market at the time.

As the company experienced meteoric growth, the two largest business units of the company, marketing and development, believing that their needs were very distinct from one another, organized separate support services. Another library resource was established to serve the technical information requirements of the software development staff. Technical specifications, authoritative books by recognized programming experts, and serial publications related to software engineering comprised the material collections of this new library. A hardware and software laboratory was created for developers for the purpose of evaluating product design and function. This library was centralized within the development group. Both library groups supported the broad information needs of their respective client communities including a quick-reference, computer-assisted library research and document delivery. In addition, the developers' library, the Technical Resource Center, produced a regular seminar program designed to bring technical experts to Lotus to speak on a variety of significant industry topics and issues. Eventually, the two groups were merged to form a large corporate library group with a comprehensive program of information services to serve the diverse and cross-functional needs of the corporation. IRG was organized around the Resource Center which housed the book, periodical, software, and hardware resources of the combined group. At peak size, the library staff included about eleven full-time professional staff members and three or four part-time library assistants.

The Transition to Virtuality, or the "Virtual Bookshelf"

As the company's rapid domestic and international growth continued, many of the library services were available only to local employees who could access the physical facilities of the Resource Center or attend a local technical seminar program. Electronic mail, in use from the beginning days of the company, allowed the library to receive information requests and to deliver results electronically, regardless of the employee's geographic location. Still, not everyone was accustomed to using electronic mail. Later, telefacsimile made delivery of certain information to remote points more feasible. Both the weekly industry newsletter and an industry news service were delivered via electronic mail to employees in offices around the world. The library even experimented with CD-ROM delivery by making an electronic collection of the library's newsletters and industry newswire announcements, as well as some other electronic data, available to Field Sales and international offices. The purpose was to offer a retrospective collection (i.e., a small "library") of these industry news services available on CD-ROM with an easy-to-use menu system and proprietary search and retrieval software. The technology needed to develop these efforts was readily available at Lotus. Lotus communications software, a Lotus search and retrieval software product, an established electronic mail infrastructure and data network, and a CD-ROM publishing operation were already in place and in use at Lotus. Many of the library's clientele were regular users of these technologies.

IRG was a full-fledged corporate library resource with all of the traditional collections and services offered by most corporations of comparable, if not larger, size, and the group had made significant strides in delivering information beyond the confines of the physical space. However, an outstanding issue complicated these electronic delivery efforts. Each project was based on disparate technical platforms with different user interfaces. A library user, for example, might be able to log onto the data network and search the library's catalog based on the library automation software chosen by the library, but would have to use another software interface when he or she wanted to search the library's newswire. Additionally, the end user might or might not have had the proper desktop computing configuration to access the needed service. In 1991 Lotus solved this problem for IRG. A corporate mandate was issued to upgrade every desktop computer with minimum requirements to run the company's newly released groupware product, Lotus Notes. All employees at Lotus were given the necessary hardware, software, and training to use Lotus Notes for all of their communication needs. The complete infrastructure now in place allowed the library to build a "virtual bookshelf." For more detail about Lotus Notes, see the article "Lotus Notes Databases: The Foundation of a Virtual Library," cited at the end of this chapter.

Why a Virtual Library Using Lotus Notes?

As in other industries, general economic trends and significant competitive pressures within the industry forced Lotus to make an extensive analysis of its cost structure in order to maximize competitiveness. IRG was not exempt from a top-down review. During this review, IRG surveyed and benchmarked itself against similar corporate libraries. The staff reviewed usage levels of all library services including the physical collections, research services, seminar series, and electronic services. It was no surprise to find that the most widely used and valued information services were customized research and all of the full-text news services that were available through electronic means.

There are several reasons why IRG made this transition to the virtual library using Lotus Notes as the unifying platform. First, the company was standardized on Lotus Notes and clients had become accustomed to desktop delivery of information using the familiar interface provided by Lotus Notes. There was a new sense of end user empowerment, that is, self-sufficiency with regard to information gathering. A wide variety of information sources available through Lotus Notes can be searched, stored, and viewed through this common interface. Second, Lotus Notes features full-text retrieval capabilities that are reasonably straightforward for the end user. A "query-builder" and form-based searches are part of the full-text search interface. These help users to enter successful search statements. The text of multiple databases can be searched simultaneously. This is especially helpful for users who are not familiar with content, but it also simplifies the effort to locate needed information from different Lotus Notes databases. Access to information services via Lotus Notes gives clients access to electronic information 24 hours a day, seven days a week. Third, a unique feature of Lotus Notes is the ability to make replica copies of individual databases. Through this replication feature, data can be synchronized in all replica copies of a database over a short period of time. This ensures the accessibility of updated information in databases which are distributed to a worldwide user base. Geographic boundaries are transcended either through this database replication feature or by virtue of the fact that Lotus Notes databases are accessible on the corporate data network. Individuals in other buildings can access databases via the local-area network connection or through a phone connection to a specified Lotus Notes database server. Fourth, because Lotus Notes is both a development and a delivery platform, new databases can be designed and information applications developed in a shorter time than with other development platforms. Fifth, the Lotus Notes development platform is relatively easy to learn; some of the database design for IRG's virtual library was accomplished by library staff. Finally, it has a database access control feature that allows IRG to authorize individuals to read a database. This security feature is necessary for keeping track of licensed users of a database.

In addition to these compelling reasons, IRG staff was downsized and the budget was reduced. IRG, therefore, needed to adopt a strategy that would allow the remaining staff members to focus maximum energy on the most valued services. In the final evaluation, IRG recommended a strategic realignment which focused on showcasing Lotus Notes to deliver electronic information services and on promoting electronic access to library-based resources.

Three new imperatives resulted from this realignment of IRG's efforts: (1) to design and build an electronic "virtual library" on the Lotus Notes platform; (2) to deliver a high-quality research service using Lotus Notes when possible; and (3) to pilot and market innovative information delivery products on the Notes platform.

The physical resources of IRG were pared down to a highly focused core collection. Books were offered to employees on a "permanent loan" basis. The software collection was handed over to the Lotus Technical Support Group. The library's collections still include magazines and newspapers, paper-based market research service, standalone CD-ROM-based information products, and videos of Lotus-produced programs and reference books — all housed in a comfortable reading and viewing area. IRG's plan for a virtual library includes Lotus Notes applications for client use and applications used by the library staff, networked CD-ROM information services, and the IRG InfoLine.

The virtual library consists of a set of information applications, or Lotus Notes databases, developed and licensed for the use of IRG's clients. These include several industry news databases: an industry news service by topic, filtered and delivered by Individual Inc. through their First! product; real-time news via Desktop Data's NewsEDGE/Notes product from several broadcast wire feeds including Dow-Vision, Knight-Ridder Tribune News, ZiffWire, and First Call; and IRG's customized Lotus newsletter, Micro News.

IRG's clients can also search and review the full text of market research reports in Lotus Notes databases from the following vendors: New Science Associates, Gartner Group, Burton Group, META Group, and Forrester Research. Company financial and other data are available to IRG's clients in several CD/Notes databases (delivered on CD-ROM in the Lotus Notes file format) from OneSource Information Services. Another Lotus Notes database is the library catalog data, which was converted from the previously used library automation system and gives views of the documents by title, author, subject, etc. An electronic version of the *Wall Street Journal*, developed and licensed by SandPoint Corporation and Dow Jones, is one of the most popular applications offered by IRG.

Other databases are in the works. Ziff-Davis's Computer Library division is preparing to release a Lotus Notes-based version of its popular CD-ROM information product, Computer Select. IRG clients will be able to access this product via Lotus Notes when available. A new phrase, "interactive publication," refers to features that allow publishers to design a database that includes a discussion forum with the full text of the publication delivered in Lotus Notes. This is exemplified by "Patricia Seybold's Notes on Information Technology," the first vendor to integrate this discussion feature along with its Lotus Notes publication. Included in each month's update is an editorial feature called "Readers' New Topic" that invites readers to comment by composing a document in the database. The readers' comments update the database and are available for other readers to respond to or make additional comments. This adds a new dimension to electronic publications.

A road map to this virtual library can be found in the Lotus Notes database called "The IRG Virtual Library Guide" (Figure 1). This database provides a description of all IRG services and allows clients to use a software "button" which, when clicked with a mouse, installs all of the IRG database icons on the client's Lotus Notes workspace (Figure 2). Clients can also use the database to fill out an electronic request form for information to be researched by IRG. Lotus Notes automatically routes this request to a tracking database monitored by IRG's research staff.

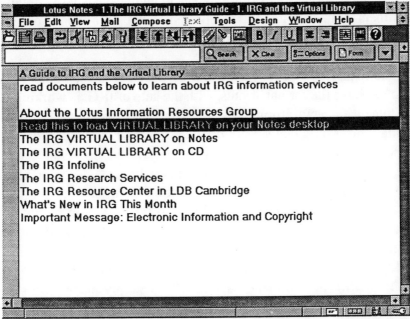

Figure 1: Main view listing documents in the IRG Virtual Library Guide database

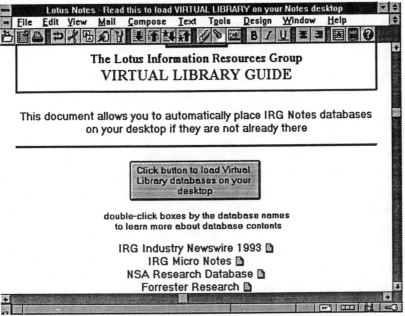

Figure 2: Document showing database install button in the IRG Virtual Library Guide database

Several other Lotus Notes applications have been designed by IRG staff for administrative purposes. These include the research-tracking database where new requests are routed from Lotus Notes electronic mail. In this database, IRG staff can monitor incoming requests, assign them to appropriate individuals, track their status, and use a variety of forms to deliver results via Lotus Notes mail. After the transaction is complete, the database serves as a repository for finished requests, providing data on who the requester was and including cost center numbers for chargeback purposes. The results of an individual research inquiry can be stored in the database for future reference. This application is critical for keeping track of chargeback transactions as well as for other usage analysis. IRG keeps track of purchase orders and invoices with Lotus Notes. The library staff record status reports using Lotus Notes and another database contains slides used by individual staff members for internal and external presentations. This method of information sharing allows IRG staff to shorten the time they take to collaborate, share results, and communicate effectively with each other and with clients.

Other pieces of the virtual library to be included when available are computer industry newsletters published in the Lotus Notes file format. Lotus, with the help of IRG, is working to encourage and support the development of new information products for delivery via Lotus Notes. For CD-ROM-based information services that are not delivered in the Lotus Notes database format, IRG plans to provide network-based access. Once available via the corporate data network, IRG's clients will be able to run these CD-ROM services from the Lotus Notes interface. A special Lotus Notes database could be designed to provide information about each of the CDs. In the same document that describes the CD-ROM-based service, a software "button" could be programmed to launch the product and bring up the user interface for searching. Once searching is complete, the interface would return to Lotus Notes.

The IRG InfoLine is an important component of the virtual library. The InfoLine is IRG's "electronic access to intelligent information agent." This simply means that clients can call the IRG InfoLine, a phone hotline, and leave voice mail describing their inquiry. IRG promises a response within 24 hours. The InfoLine is also an electronic mailbox that is programmed to receive standard Lotus Notes mail messages from IRG's clients around the world.

Impact of the Virtual Library on IRG and Other Issues

The virtual library enables IRG's clients to gather information and answer questions at their desktop. The type of information that IRG's clients can access includes general business and financial news and data, company information, information on products, and information on technologies. The impact on IRG's research services is that staff members are available to deal with incremental inquiries and work on more sophisticated and complex research projects. IRG's transition to the virtual library has required staff and information providers to work through licensing issues that relate to Lotus Notes value-added software and original information content. IRG has negotiated pricing and contracts for many of these services. Pricing and copyright are complex matters which are still in an evolutionary stage. IRG staff have worked with several vendors to develop rational pricing models and licensing arrangements. Copyright protection of electronic information is a serious concern for IRG and its clients. IRG takes a proactive role in raising the awareness of these issues at Lotus and in pursuing solutions that serve as a model for Lotus customers.

The IRG information specialists have had to develop new technical skills, including Lotus Notes database design and administration, in order to be more knowledgeable in implementing, developing, and deploying the services of the virtual library. What was formerly called collection development and maintenance in the traditional library has shifted to new activities which include selecting external wire services and other electronically published data, negotiating licenses and contracts, database administration, and hardware and software troubleshooting. IRG staff are now prepared to train end users to take full advantage of the portfolio of information services available to them electronically. Clients need training particularly in using Lotus Notes for full-text retrieval, in setting up customized profiles, and in understanding database content.

IRG's Impact on Lotus: Challenges and Opportunities

IRG was one of the earliest groups to use Lotus Notes. Having pioneered the effort to bring external information into Lotus Notes, IRG has been recognized at Lotus as content and publishing experts. IRG continues to play a leadership role by demonstrating the creative uses of the full-text retrieval interface and search engine which is part of Lotus Notes. Design features in Lotus Notes can be exploited to provide new approaches to customized topic alert services, electronic clipping files, and other information-filtering capabilities. IRG's information specialists will develop these approaches and train clients to use them effectively.

Information gaps not filled by Lotus Notes can be made available through the use of networked CD-ROMs. IRG intends to provide a desktop interface to some of the CD-ROM products that can fill these gaps.

IRG will explore additional published resources which can be made available through Lotus Notes, encouraging and supporting publishers when possible. As other Lotus Notes customers express interest, IRG will support and encourage efforts to develop library automation applications that work with Lotus Notes. Opportunities for Lotus Notes interfaces to the Internet will also be pursued. Since Lotus Notes supports both document imaging and multimedia, IRG will apply these technologies to the virtual library as appropriate. During the past year, IRG has showcased the use of Lotus Notes in the library setting. Meetings will continue with information specialists in large corporations that are Lotus Notes customers. IRG plays a valuable role in demonstrating to customers the information-sharing opportunities presented by Lotus Notes.

In this new environment, the challenge for IRG is to maintain contact with internal customers and to stay in tune with their information needs. Because much of the interaction with these individuals is electronic, IRG must find new ways to interact directly and indirectly. Methods to be used include a sophisticated usage-tracking database that monitors all of IRG's other databases to find out who the users are and what information they are using. Electronic mail surveys will also be sent. Monthly worldwide electronic mail messages will announce new services and highlight existing ones. Staff will visit with clients to provide orientation and assist them in personalizing information filters. IRG's goal is to provide services that are so valued by users that they could not easily do their jobs without them. To the extent we are successful in achieving this goal, IRG's cost of doing business will continue to be supported by the end users through chargeback and other funding models.

One of the most significant results of the shift in IRG's strategy is that the group, while concerned primarily with providing critical information to Lotus decision-makers, has aligned itself more closely with the company's business. IRG has become an important team player by demonstrating the information advantages and productivity gains from deploying Lotus Notes.

References

1. Brodwin, David, et al. "The Delivery and Distribution of Information in a Client/Server World: A Report on the Technology Trends Altering the Way People Obtain and Share Information in an Organization." Cambridge: Arthur D. Little, 1992.
2. Liberman, Kristen, and Jane L. Rich. "Lotus Notes Databases: The Foundation of a Virtual Library," *Database,* 16(3), June 1993, pp. 33-46.

Chapter 13
How to Make Information Technology Work for You
Monica Ertel

I once had a boss who was fond of sharing quotes with me from his homeland of France. One of the first things he said to me as we began to talk about library services at Apple was: "Déplacer le tabouret vers le piano."

This means "Move the bench to the piano." I've kept this quote in a visible place in my office ever since then because I think that it contains a very important message. It means that we as information professionals cannot wait for people to come to us; we must reach out to our customer base and deliver information in a proactive manner. We can no longer expect that our clients and companies will tolerate a passive information service. We must move the library toward our users rather than expecting them to come to us. In other words, we should not be trying to move the piano when we should be concentrating on moving the bench.

We are witnessing some very challenging times. Our organizations are in the process of reinventing themselves. They are facing fierce global competition, a sluggish economy, and a rapidly changing marketplace. Our libraries are not immune from these challenges. We find ourselves being asked to do more with less, to downsize our staffs, cut our budgets, justify our existence, compete with vendors offering information services directly to our clients, and sometimes even compete with other departments within our organizations to deliver information. Information and how it is leveraged will become a critical success factor for business survival in the global economic web.

How are we going to respond to these challenges? What are we going to do to justify our existence? How can we prove our value to our institutions and organizations? As the noted 1960's radical Eldridge Cleaver said, "You're either part of the solution or part of the problem." I believe the key lies in how we deliver information to our clients. How we use information technology to do this is what this chapter will discuss.

Someone recently told me that the Chinese character for warning is a combination of the characters for danger and opportunity. Perhaps this character should be adopted as the official logo for libraries today. We are in a time like no other. For the first time in more than a hundred years, we face the magnificent challenge of redesigning library services. We have a greater opportunity to bring service to wherever the potential users of library services happen to be. We have the increased power of technology to improve access to and delivery of information. With fewer resources and increased demands, we face the danger of not being able to meet our users' needs and expectations. We face the danger of someone else filling this need and leaving us in the dust. However, we also face the opportunity of forever changing the role of the corporate library into a vital and essential part of our company's business strategy. And so we have to proceed with caution as we enter this new age of information services. But we cannot let this caution make us hesitate to accept this opportunity.

Definition of Information Systems

Michael Buckland gives the following provocative quote in his book *Information and Information Systems* as the goal of a worthy information system:

> [It should] give sense to its collections, make learning easier, stimulate curiosity, help to avoid pure memorizing which is so detrimental to independent thinking and self-reliance, and fill more and more the harmful gap between formal concepts and intuition, theory and practice.[1]

I call this quote provocative because it was made in 1811 by Habsburg Archduke Johann when he established an institution in Graz to encourage education and industrial competitiveness in Styria. Information systems are simply the combined interaction between the user and the information provider and the systems which transmit the information. Textbook definitions of information systems generally include the following:

> A system is an integration of parts, all contributing to the achievement of an overall goal. It supports the managers and employees and key environmental elements by furnishing information in the proper time frame to assist in decision making.[2]

Most libraries utilize retrieval-based information systems which facilitate access to information and support the mission of whoever funds them.[3] Information systems does not mean the use of computers in libraries. Rather it means understanding the real managerial and organizational needs of the corporation and designing a system to meet these needs. It means designing a system which helps groups of people work together more effectively. As R. I. Tricker states in his book on information management, "A manager does not have to be an electronics engineer to use the telephone. He does, however, have to appreciate the available services and know what is required of him."[4] So, too, do librarians in today's information arena. We do not necessarily have to be systems programmers but we must have a very clear understanding of our users' needs, available information resources, and how we want to deliver those resources to the users. Information systems themselves are useless without an effective relationship between the people who provide the service and the people who use the service.

A Brief History of Information Technology in Libraries

The history of information technology in libraries can be divided into four main events or revolutions. The first computerized information retrieval systems as we know them today made their appearance in libraries in the early 1960s. Large mainframes, which required their own special air-conditioned rooms and technical staffs, managed the catalogs of large institutions — generally university libraries. Because of the huge costs and resources required to maintain this type of system, only a few of the largest libraries could afford to take advantage of this technology.

Personal computers began to appear in libraries in the late 1970s and early 1980s. This caused a revolution in information technology in libraries because it was now possible for even the smallest library to automate some of their processes, such as catalog card production and circulation control. A study sponsored by the U.S. Department of Education in December 1978 indicated that some libraries were using "miniature computers" to assist in circulation, acquisition, serials control, reference, administration, and audiovisual services.[5] Another study indicated that by 1984 an estimated 81 percent of libraries were using some sort of personal computer in their libraries.[6]

The next revolution was the advent in the late 1980s of local-area networking within our organizations. Initially a library could network all the workstations within the library, allowing staff to communicate with one another and share data from common file servers. Eventually libraries were able to offer their services on the network beyond the confines of the physical library, making the concept of the "library without walls" a reality. A 1987 nationwide study of 600 libraries and information centers by the Queens College Graduate School of Library and Information Studies indicated that data sharing, electronic mail, uploading and downloading, device sharing, and software sharing were the most significant reasons for using local-area networks in libraries and information centers.[7]

The latest revolution has been the ability to deliver personalized information to our clients' desktops. There is an increasing need for personalized, in-context, timely information. There is also a tremendous growth in the availability of external and internal information, and the arrival of many enabling technologies is making it possible for us to deliver this information on an individualized basis. No longer do our patrons have to come to our libraries to obtain the information they need to do their jobs; nor do they even have to log onto our libraries' databases. They want and expect to have the information they need delivered to their personal desktops. In addition, with cutbacks in library staff and closure of branch libraries, desktop availability of external databases has become even more critical. In one case, the closure of two branch libraries within a corporation resulted in more than a 60 percent increase in the number of logins to the library's databases from individual desktops.[8]

In short, it is not sufficient to have a centralized information service which we expect our customers to use. We now must actively go out to our customers, determine what they want, and deliver it in a personalized way. Our value to our organizations will not be measured by the number of items in our collections, the variety of databases we offer, the extent of our periodical collections, or even the number of services we offer on the network. Our value will be measured by the accuracy, relevance, and speed with which we deliver information directly to our users, no matter where they reside.

A Look Ahead

Before we look at specific examples or discuss specifics about implementing an effective information system it may be helpful to envision what library usage could possibly be like in the next decade. Imagine the following scenario in the year 2004:

An engineer is working on the next generation of speech recognition. She has been kept up-to-date on the latest developments in her field by a twice-daily news report which is delivered to her personal digital assistant no matter where she happens to be located that day. This news contains not only text but also video, sound, and graphics. As the engineer begins to write a paper for a conference where she will be presenting a paper on her research, she decides to get some background information on one of the other speakers on her panel. She docks into the company's information services network by wireless access and pulls up a biography on the panelist, an interview done on CNN, and a list of papers and patents authored by this person. The engineer requests the full text of several of the papers from the network and downloads these to her electronic notebook, noting that all copyright charges have been duly paid. She then decides to find a quote by the company president to start out her talk and searches an internal database built and indexed by the library staff. She receives a list of possible quotes, ranked by relevance, and quickly determines the most appropriate line to use in her speech. Finally, she pulls up information on restaurants in the conference city and makes a reservation by e-mail. Note that the engineer is in Singapore and the company library is in Boston. How is this going to affect our libraries? Are we prepared to meet this scenario? And how will we make this happen?

What Is the Library's Role?

As information systems have moved from the large centralized computing centers down to our desktops, so has the responsibility for implementing these types of systems in our libraries. In the 1960s, we could assign the responsibility for building and maintaining these systems to the Management Information Systems (MIS) group or central computing facilities. Because libraries were not always considered to be of prime importance to these organizations, we often found that we were the last to be helped and that important activities such as updating our large databases were often relegated to the bottom of the pile. With personal computers, we were able to gain more control over these processes. We no longer had to rely on the MIS group to keep our databases up-to-date. We could easily and quickly maintain the data that the library created and disseminated to our users. With the advent of networking, our patrons could now access our collections without actually coming into the library.

The latest developments are requiring that we be more proactive than ever before, that we deliver personalized information to our users' desktops. Delivery to the desktop has required much more expertise and many more resources than simply maintaining our databases on personal computers within our libraries. We are dealing with reduced budgets, restricted staffing, rising costs, increased technological complexity, expensive and tricky database licensing issues, and rising demands. How are we going to build the systems necessary to deliver this information? How are we going to balance our lack of resources and the increased demand? How will we build systems to meet the future needs of our clients such as the engineer described above? We are almost back to the situation when the information systems revolution began in libraries: we need to work with other organizations within our corporations and institutions in order to make this feasible. Building partnerships with other parts of our organization and helping our staffs develop new and different skills are going to be vital to our future success.

A Look Inside

One way to illustrate what has happened and what is ahead in implementing effective information systems in our libraries is to discuss a couple of examples from libraries and information centers that have successfully implemented information technology. My focus is on the Apple Library because this is the example I am most familiar with and I use two examples because there is no one way to go about establishing partnerships or offering quality information services. Depending on an organization's goals and values, the approach and results will vary. It cannot be overemphasized that it is extremely important to know your organization's goals and values before you attempt to design an information delivery system.

The Apple Library was established in 1981 as a very small, one-person engineering library. Because of the company's business, it was expected that the library would rapidly achieve a fairly high level of automation using the company's product, an Apple II personal computer. A list of the fledgling periodical collection was entered into a simple word processor and easily printed as new titles were added. As simple as this sounds, it was a major change from the way periodical lists had been done in the past. At my previous employer, this list was given to the centralized word processing group which entered the data and formatted it. It often took up to eight weeks to get the list back from this group. Needless to say, it was not updated more than once or twice a year. It was a major improvement to be able to gain control over this fairly simple process.

By 1986, the library had grown to eight employees and had a very efficient Macintosh local-area network within the group. They shared a couple of laser printers and began to use a messaging system called QuickMail within the group. This system cut down dramatically on the number of paper memos they produced as well as improved communication within the group because of the ease with which they could "talk" to one another.

By 1989, library employees had set up several servers within the library and began to offer some services over the network, such as access to some public domain software and some internally generated databases. In 1990, the library began to offer network access to CD-ROMs containing bibliographic and graphic data. Up to this point, library staff were able to do all of this utilizing the expertise of the staff and the resources of their department. They did not have to go outside the library group to make this happen. However, it began to get more complicated as they endeavored to make more information available via the company network.

By 1990, it was apparent to the Apple Library that in order to maximize the use of services, the library needed to better integrate the delivery of its information services with some of the groups within the company who had larger-scale information delivery operations. AppleLink is the main corporate-wide information delivery system at Apple. It is available to employees in all parts of the world and includes everything from electronic forms to press releases, from product information to corporate policies to discussion groups. The Apple Library felt that it was important to have a presence on this medium because it would allow the library to make its services available to any Apple employee anywhere in the world. From a survey of library customers' needs, the library knew that this was one of their main concerns and thus it became one of the library's top priorities. The first step was to contact the AppleLink group which reported to another part of the organization. The library held a series of meetings and began to negotiate for space on this system. At the time, space was limited and the library had to sell its idea to the AppleLink group. But once the library showed the group the types of content the library wanted to provide, the various statistics kept on usage, and their projections for future use, the library was seen as a very attractive addition to this information service. Responsibility for updating the Apple Library folder on AppleLink has been assigned to one person in the library who acts as a coordinator for the various types of information provided by the different departments within the library. In addition, because AppleLink also functions as Apple's in-house e-mail system, the library is able to send personalized SDIs directly to employees' individual e-mail boxes.

It has been a very satisfactory relationship because the Apple Library has been able to update its own databases while AppleLink maintains the overall system. Employees worldwide are able to access information, such as new reports, access their current awareness bulletins, and check out new library services. In addition, AppleLink has gained some very useful and popular content for its service.

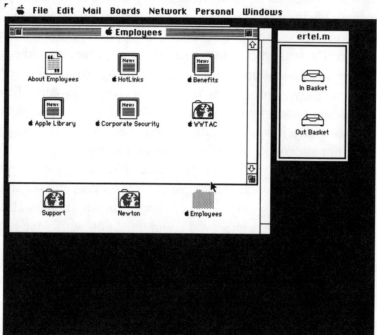

Figure 1: AppleLink: View of information available in the Employees' section of AppleLink, Apple's corporate-wide information delivery system.

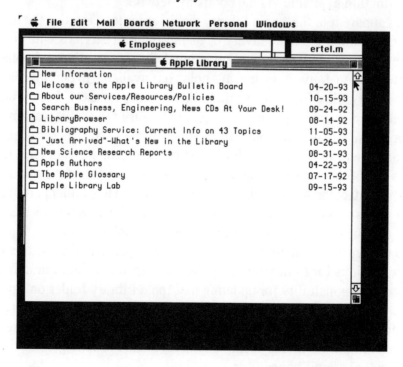

Figure 2: AppleLink: Apple Library information contained within the Employees' section of AppleLink.

About the same time, the Apple Library wanted to offer access to several CD-ROMs over the network; however, it was not possible for the Library to do this via AppleLink. AppleLink is a standalone information service, where the content is provided in a format governed by AppleLink. It cannot be used as a front end to databases such as CD-ROMs or other external databases not specially formatted for AppleLink. This presented a dilemma to the library because its goal was to provide as much access to its resources as possible without requiring employees to come into the physical library—or in the words of the library's Vice President, "move the bench to piano." The library believed that networked access to the CD-ROM network was an essential part of how it wanted to deliver information to Apple employees.

About the same time that the library was negotiating with AppleLink to deliver library information, another group was dealing with the issue of providing access to server-based information. This was an excellent solution to the Apple library's CD-ROM network problem. The library staff set up a series of meetings with this group, Engineering Computer Operations (ECO), to discuss how the library could take advantage of this medium. Although this server-based network is not available to all employees, unlike AppleLink which is available to any employee in San Francisco or Kuala Lumpur, it does reach most of the research and development staff who are the network's main customers. In a short time, the library has become the largest information provider on this network and has had a great deal of support from this group. Additionally, ECO has learned a lot about running an active information service, gaining new appreciation for the type of service libraries provide to employees.

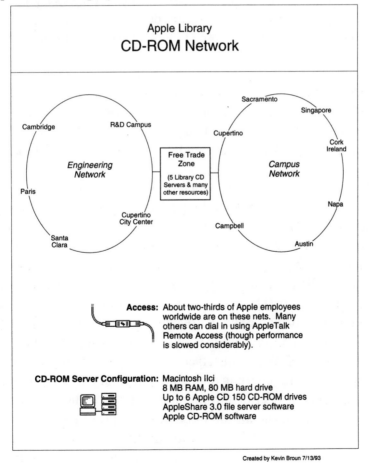

Figure 3: Map of the Apple Library's CD ROM Network

With the rapid changes taking place daily in most industries, access to immediate information is extremely important. Newswires have become an increasingly important vehicle for providing quick and instant access to news almost as it happens. Beginning in 1992, the Apple Library began to experiment with delivering daily news to top executives at Apple Computer. Using a wire service called First!,[9] the library has built a profile of interests, using several key words. The news is delivered to the library over the Internet every night. Working with one of its software groups, the library wrote a short program which takes this information and delivers it via e-mail to forty executives each morning. It is interesting that the library got help from this software group not because it asked them but rather because the group approached the library about getting access to this information. The library has had some fascinating feedback regarding this service. One day, the service sent subscribers this note :

> Based upon the current definition of your profile, SMART has determined that there were no stories in the current news traffic that met your minimum criteria of relevance.

The library staff was delighted to see the following message posted on company e-mail that day:

> In my mind, the most useful thing that has happened to me, with respect to the use of information, is this wonderful message I got today from my "customized news agent" that normally delivers 12 news articles to me each day. I wish I could get more of these messages. What a great time saver!

This example illustrates that, at times, it may be as important for us to act as filters of information, so that no information is delivered, as it is for us for find information for our clients. Our roles will become even more valuable if our clients trust us to filter information for them, ensuring that they get only the information they need and want, but leaving the door open for additional exploration if they desire.

Now that the Apple Library is able to offer a wide variety of information services to employees via several networks, the issue becomes how do the users know what is available and how do they figure out how to use these services. The Apple Library now has more than a dozen information resources available on the network--an electronic ocean of information. But it also has almost as many interfaces for people to navigate as well as information in several locations.

This is where the challenge really begins. It is not enough to get information up on the network—for employee access—to expand the walls of the library. Libraries need to make it easy for their clients to find what is available and to use what the libraries have to offer. But this requires a rather technical skill-set which many of us do not have on our staffs. It requires some sophisticated programming and knowledge of human interface design and network protocols. Many libraries today are hiring systems librarians reporting directly to the library director or manager to coordinate and implement this important aspect of information services. Many libraries have restrictions placed on their staffing levels and cannot add these important staff members to their ranks. If they do have the positions, they cannot find anyone to fill the job. Systems Librarian is one of the hottest jobs in libraries today and the competition for these employees is fierce.

How do we proceed in the face of these restrictions? It is going to be increasingly important for us to form partnerships with other groups within our organizations in order to get the assistance we need or to emphasize a different set of skills in the staff we hire.

The Apple Library is working on a project called Database Launcher. This project is spearheaded by an information specialist who has spent a great deal of time learning programming skills and dedicating a portion of his time to working on his new skill. He has designed a HyperCard interface to the Apple Library's networked CD-ROMs which allows an employee to look in one place to determine what information is available and to "launch" a specific CD-ROM. The user can then search the CD-ROM using each CD's specific interface. It also allows the user to automatically place document requests and to give feedback about this service. It does not solve the problem of one unified search language for all of the CDs but it is a first step toward solving this issue. Users now only have to go to one place to find what resources are available to them through the Apple Library.

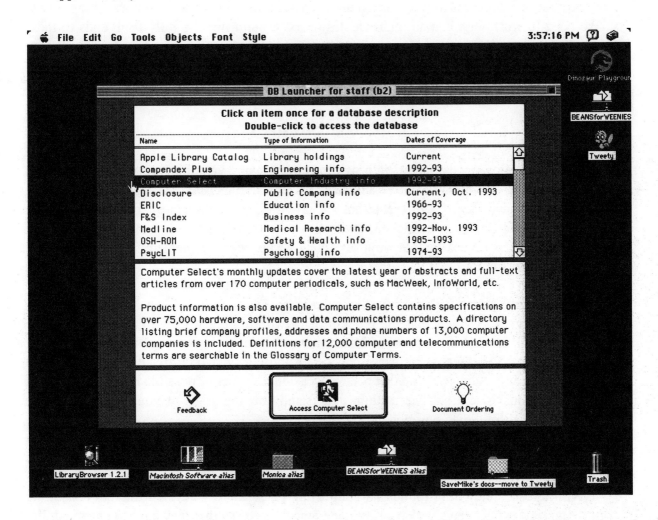

Figure 4: Database Launcher

What does the future hold for information delivery at Apple? Apple has a project, Personal Apple Library or PAL, which looks at the issue of designing one unified front end to all of the varied information resources available from the library. It is not enough to make information available over the network if employees cannot figure out how to use the variety of interfaces or figure out where to go to get the information. We must make it as straightforward as possible to figure out what resources are available.

In the days before networking, a patron walked through the doors of the library, approached the reference desk, and asked a friendly human being for assistance. Our information systems need to be as simple and approachable as the friendly human. Instead, now we expect our users to log onto the network and somehow stumble upon the entrance to this rich world of resources. Once they find the key to the door, they are expected to know a variety of languages to find an answer to their quest.

Just because information is available electronically over a network does not mean that our goal to provide global access to information has been accomplished. We still have a long way to go. We need to work with human interface designers to build user-friendly front ends to these information sources. We need to work with our corporate computer centers to make sure that we are included in corporate-wide information delivery systems and we need to build new skill-sets in our staffs so that they can be active players in designing and building these systems for our clients.

Success Factors

What are the major success factors in providing effective and valuable information systems to our users in the face of limited resources and lack of technical expertise? Keep in mind that there is no one right way to proceed. Different libraries have different approaches, all of which may be quite successful. Establishing partnerships within our organizations and developing our staffs are two key factors. Keep in mind the following key points as you look at implementing any information system within your library,

- *Support from your MIS or computing support group is crucial.* Jean Martin at MCC in Austin, Texas, believes that the process of networking software will work much more smoothly if one has the support of MIS or a member of one's own staff who is technically competent. She offers some useful advice for those trying to cultivate the support of an unhelpful MIS manager: send that person occasional articles of possible interest, invite him or her to lunch, and help her or him understand how the goals of your library meet the overall goals of the corporation.

  Richard Geiger at the *San Francisco Chronicle* says that working with the MIS group is their only hope for being able to acquire certain software customizations which help his group provide information to editors or reporters.

  At Microsoft, they have found that contracting for services with their internal consulting organization has been a very positive experience. They say that they have to pay top dollar for this service, as would any other customer, but that the performance and follow-through have been tremendous. Working with the MIS group has made them understand the value of the product and how it will benefit more than one organization within the company.

At a major telecommunication company, the computer center is moving toward a client/server environment, which means that groups providing the actual content will be able to assume more responsibility for actually mounting and updating their information. As employees from all levels demand direct access to information, the MIS departments are designing more user-friendly systems and are looking for content. Libraries are now being seen as very attractive partners in many cases because they have the access to this content. It is going to be important to leverage this desire for content into assistance in developing our delivery systems.

- *Educate the computer support groups within your organization.* At Bolt Beranek and Newman (Cambridge, Massachusetts), Marian Bremer, library manager, suggests having lunch regularly with the various managers and top staff people of the departments whose assistance you need. She schedules time in staff meetings to describe the library's goals for the year, and talks to managers whenever she knows that something the library wants will impact them. She says that this has been a learning experience on both sides and that it is an ongoing effort to make sure the computer support groups and the library understand each other's needs. BBN has also started a library technical advisory board with representatives from a range of computer support groups within the organization, plus managers from BBN's information technology division. This has been very useful, not just for library projects, but as a way for some of the groups to understand how diverse information-related projects overlap.

- *Develop specialties within your staff.* Specialties within the library staff are not only desirable but necessary as libraries become more deeply involved in electronic information delivery. Librarians must know their computer systems well enough to understand what is possible and their clients well enough to know what they want.
Bremer has her staff specialize in different platforms: the database administrator specializes in VAX/VMS and Macintosh applications; the PC specialist in DOS, Windows, and CD-ROMs; Bremer herself specializes in Internet and Unix issues. She and her staff understand that it is important to be able to "talk the talk" to some degree, so that her library can effectively work with other departments to deliver first-class information services.
As Suzi Hayes at Encore Computer Corporation puts it, it can be very frustrating to deal with the lack of support from the MIS group but "it is very satisfying to know that when the project is done, you did most of the work yourself, really understood how it works, and lived to tell about it."

- *Hire a systems librarian if possible.* Bremer also says that she sees a great benefit to the library's having its own system support person, although at BBN this has not been possible. Sometimes the library can be seen as demanding too much support but once the computer support group understands why the library's goals are important to the company as a whole, it can be a wonderful ally. And it gives these groups good exposure as well if they are involved in effective and worthwhile projects.
Amy Howard at Bellcore says that several library staff members have focused on becoming more knowledgeable in the systems area. They have been quite successful, but since they all have other duties as well, it would probably be better if one person could focus his or her efforts instead of having this as a more diffuse effort.

Richard Geiger at The *San Francisco Chronicle* says that having a systems person reporting to the library, even if primarily as an advocate, is extremely valuable. He says that having someone report directly to the library gives your group real results, quickly and within your priorities.

- *Get a sponsor.* Try to find a champion within the organization to assist you in implementing your system. Many libraries have found that it helps to find someone who is excited about your project and who can help facilitate things, since library functions typically are not given as high a priority as we expect or are viewed as being far simpler to implement than they really are.

- *Be persistent!* The libraries that have established effective information systems have done so because they have been stubborn in their pursuit. They have worked hard to understand the technical issues themselves and have not been discouraged by the initial lack of interest from departments they consider crucial to the successful implementation of their projects. They have stuck in there and not given up until they found someone who could help them or have learned how to do it themselves.
As Geiger at The *San Francisco Chronicle* puts it, his library has succeeded in involving other groups to help his group deliver information by lots of phone calls, cajoling, and even a little nagging.

- *Give credit where credit is due.* Finally, it is important to give credit to departments who have provided you with valuable assistance. Everyone loves to be recognized and given positive exposure. So, if the computer operations group helps you mount a new service, be sure to announce it as "The library and Computer Operations present...." This may go a long ways toward getting help the next time you ask.

Conclusion

In these critical times, it is more important to leverage our expertise and resources. Our roles can become even more valuable if we meet the critical business needs of our corporations. Utilizing the latest information technology, taking advantage of our expertise as information providers, and establishing partnerships with key groups within our organizations, we can be essential players as we deliver information to our users and as we look ahead to designing effective systems for the future.

References

1. Buckland, Michael. *Information and Information Systems.* New York: Praeger, 1991, p. 36.
2. McLeod, Raymond. *Management Information Systems.* Chicago: SRA, 1986, p. 17.
3. Buckland, Michael. *Information and Information Systems.* New York, Praeger, 1991, P 30.
4. Tricker, R. I. *Effective Information Management.* Oxford, England, Beaumont Executive Press, 1982, P 2.
5. Simpson, George A. *Microcomputers in Library Automation.* USDHEW, 1978, MITRE-TR 7938. Available from ERIC.
6. *Micromomputers in ACRL Libraries.* Association of Research Libraries. Washington, D.C., May 1984.
7. Kibirige, Harry. Local-area networks in an Online Information Retrieval Environment. Proceedings of the 9th National Online Meeting, New York, May 10-12, 1988.
8. Personal correspondence with Amy Howard, Bellcore, November 9, 1993.
9. First! is available from Individual Inc., 1499 Bayshore Highway #203, Burlingame, CA 94010. (415) 259-9900 or fax (415) 259-9902.

Chapter 14
Developing a Multi-Platform CD-ROM Network at Bolt, Beranek and Newman
Bobb Menk and David Escalante

Introduction

Bolt, Beranek and Newman, Inc., based in Cambridge, Massachusetts, designs and sells computer support systems including wide-area communication networks, data analysis software, and voice recognition systems; and offers consulting, research, development, and systems-building services in computers and formation physical sciences. We have approximately 1600 employees.

The Library reports to the Internet Services Division of BBN Systems and Technology, and provides research services in such diverse research areas as wide area networks, voice recognition, artificial intelligence, acoustics, software development and science education. The Library and the Computer Support departments worked jointly on the CD-ROM networking project from the summer of 1992 to the present.

Reasons for Undertaking the Project

The manager of the BBN Library, Marian Bremer, has continually searched for ways to make all types of information resources more readily available to the corporation as a whole. A very traditional way of proven value has been for the Library staff to make regular presentations about its services to other departments within the company. That very traditional format has always given us invaluable patron input for new service development.

One of the most common questions at these presentations has always been "why can't I get to stuff from my desktop?" The online catalog has long been available that way, but we felt that that was not enough. In response, we began several projects aimed at putting even more library resources on the desktops of our clients. The largest of these was our networked CD-ROM initiative, which began in June of 1992.

While the other projects are not within the scope of this chapter, it is worth noting that they are not unrelated. For example, both our current Gopher server, and our proposed Mosaic server, give prominent place to instructions for connecting to the CD-ROM databases. We hope that as these various technologies mature, we'll be able to link these projects to one another directly. Gopher and Mosaic users could then just point and click for access to our CD-ROMs or our library catalog, creating a "seamless" information resource for the entire corporation. While that day is still in the future, the links between these various networked resources provide a solid base upon which we can build.

Networking the CD-ROMs provided an attractive starting point for expanding electronic library services for several reasons.

1. The demand for the information was already there.
2. The search interfaces were already familiar to many patrons from using them in the Library.
3. The technology was mature enough to expect a reasonable level of success.
4. The CD-ROM collection was still small enough to allow a certain flexibility for product choice in such an experiment.
5. Most people in the corporation were already on one or another of our networks.
6. Success would make Library services more visible within the company.
7. We were consolidating our two main libraries into one new location. Networked access to the CD-ROM databases could help to alleviate some inconveniences resulting from the move.
8. It appeared "do-able" within our planned budget for the coming year.
9. BBN has a long history of innovative solutions to networking problems. Corporate pride was involved.

The principal challenges for the project lay in two related areas:

1. Our users work on multiple platforms, principally Macintosh, UNIX, & DOS. There are a variety of systems connecting these machines and their respective networks. Our complex network topology eliminated most "off the shelf" solutions for the project since they're mainly designed for more straightforward LAN networks made up strictly of PCs.
2. The vast majority of CD-ROM applications are written only for the DOS platform. The majority of BBN staff use Macintoshes. Running an application designed for one platform on another can be complicated and the results are not always satisfactory.

Opening Phase

Selection of CD-ROMs

Because UNIX CD-ROM applications are comparatively rare, we concentrated our initial efforts on providing access to the DOS and Macintosh platforms.

It is important to remember that this project was conceived as continually growing and changing in shape and scope. We wanted to avoid getting locked in to any specific collection of databases. Whenever we have found an affordable product to be superior to one already in use, we have not hesitated to switch.

At the start of the project, our libraries had a collection of nine CD-ROM products, all running under DOS. They included a general encyclopedia, various indexes and abstracts for industry standards, indexes of engineering and scientific reports and our two most popular databases: Computer Select, and Disclosure Compact SEC.

The collection was divided between two locations, with Computer Select installed in one library on an AT-class machine with a Sony CD player, and all of the others running in another library on a 386-SX computer using a mini-disk changer capable of holding up to six discs.

Early investigations showed that the network licensing fees for many of these products would be far more than our budget could bear. Therefore we intended from the outset to make available only our most heavily used databases. Any others that we could afford would be added as the project progressed.

Our first choices were obvious to us: Computer Select and Compact Disclosure SEC. Computer Select covers mainly the trade press for the computing industry, plus provides product information on hardware and software. Compact Disclosure provides data from corporate SEC filings.

Both got heavy use, a reasonable number of clients were already familiar with the search interfaces, and they were of interest to enough people to create a sort of "critical mass" of users to give the project an impetus for future growth. Offering one "technical" database and one "business" database gave something to each of our principal client groups. Finally, both applications are complete on one CD each, so there would be no additional technical problems caused by the need for disk switching.

A bit later in the project, as the financing became clearer, we decided to search for an index to general business literature as well, since it would fill a gap in our collection and serve the interests of nearly all of our clientele. The product we chose covered most of the major business press and had excellent indexing, though in the end its lack of any full text records proved a significant drawback.

As it turned out, our budget for the initial year of the project also allowed us to add Disclosure Worldscope, the international companion to Disclosure Compact SEC database.

As in most projects, much of what we decided to undertake depended upon decisions taken in the past. Users already knew and valued Computer Select and Disclosure. Our new offerings complemented them and reflected the kinds of data that people had been asking for most often.

Choosing among all the possible databases meant mainly deciding which ones we could afford. The price of database network licenses was one of the few readily determinable costs as we began to develop an estimated budget for what we intended to accomplish.

Estimating a Budget

Our principal justification for adding this entire project to the Library's budget was that to do so would forestall the installation of separate, smaller, departmental CD-ROM networks within the company, insuring an economy of scale to the corporation as a whole. Further, centralizing these resources in a corporate-wide resource such as the Library would provide the widest possible access to the databases.

Since some of our standalone databases were conjointly purchased with the resources of multiple departments, we built on those prior agreements to make more funding available to cover our starting costs. In the end, we garnered approximately $40,000 to cover our share of the entire cost of the project.

Obviously, as with any complex project, cost was a critical factor. Once we had negotiated what we hoped would be adequate funding into our budget, the two main remaining cost variables were simply the price of whatever hardware and software proved necessary to run the CD's over the network, and the price of our database subscription fees and their concomitant network licensing charges.

Since we hadn't yet decided how to carry out the project technically, the only possible first step was to find out how much network licensing would cost for our existing databases.

Network licensing is complex. Different vendors take different approaches. Most of the vendors we spoke to charged by the number of concurrent users using the database at any given time. Others wanted to charge based on the total number of potential users within the company. Still others charged nothing unless we intended to provide access beyond the confines of our Cambridge office complex. The network license quotes we solicited ranged from $19,000 for two concurrent users for a business and financial database, to nothing at all for an index to general business literature.

Our initial estimates indicated that five concurrent users would generally serve our user population. With cost estimates in hand, the next step was to choose the best way to provide networked access to our database subscribers so that we could develop a reasonable estimate for the rest of our costs.

At this point, we enlisted the expertise and support of our Computer Support department. Working closely with them proved to be very valuable to both parties. Without their technical expertise, the project would never have succeeded. Without the Library's determination to expand its offerings, it may never have gotten off the ground.

Exploring Terminal Emulation

Because our library catalog runs on a VAX, and since VT-100 emulation seems ubiquitous, our initial investigation centered on ways to connect a CD-ROM server to a VAX, allowing all platforms to reach it via terminal emulation. We hoped to create one electronic address to which all users could go, where they would be presented with a selection of library tools that would include our online catalog and our CD-ROM collection.

In the summer of 1992, there were two main competitors providing a terminal emulation solution. Both products are gateways connecting a CD-ROM server directly to a VAX. The hardware part for each consists of a group of PCs housed in a single case, connecting the CD-ROMs to the VAX. The software portion is installed on the VAX, runs under VMS, the VAX operating system, and "translates" the output of the hardware portion into VT-100 codes that are in turn sent to the end user's machine. End users then emulate a VAX terminal to run the VMS "translation" software. This means that both ends of the connection do some form of emulation.

To evaluate these two products, the vendors came to our offices and set up their systems for us to try. We also searched traditional published literature and the archives of the CDROMLAN electronic discussion list for reviews and information on similar projects attempted by others. Via the CDROMLAN discussion list, we solicited the opinions and experiences of those had worked with the two products. Finally, we visited the sites of some who had installed them locally, or discussed their impressions over the phone when a site visit proved inconvenient.

Upon examination of these products, some significant problems with our entire approach to the problem became evident. Terminal emulation gives access to the CD-ROMs using a "lowest common denominator" approach. Any graphics are lost, keyboards may act in unexpected ways, and parts of the screen can become invisible. The difficulties involved began to look formidable.

We had anticipated some keyboard problems. Since keyboards are not standard across platforms, an obvious problem is telling which keys mean what to the CD-ROM program. For example, what do you press when the program says "Press Esc to Quit" and you don't have an "Esc" key on your keyboard?

The most common solution to this problem is to create a small program to add to the terminal emulation program that "maps" the standard DOS keys to specific places on the standard keyboards for other platforms. Once these keyboard maps are in place, each user loads the appropriate map for their platform and then uses the CD-ROM.

However, beyond the software mapping that tells the computer which keys are which, the user also needs a map. This usually takes the form of a template on the user's keyboard as a reminder of which keys have new names when using the CD-ROMs. Creating all these maps would be a bother, but it would only need to be done at the start of the project.

Unfortunately, in our live trials, using vendor-supplied mapping and emulation software, neither we nor the vendors could make even our native VT terminals work properly with the CD-ROMs. This was discouraging to say the least.

An unanticipated problem arose from the fact that DOS applications use a 25-line screen, while VT-100 screens use only 24 lines. All the applications we hoped to network placed significant keystroke information on the bottom line of the screen. The programs were all that more difficult to use when this information was no longer visible. Using a terminal emulation solution meant we would have to devise some kind of keyboard toggle switch to go back and forth between the top and bottom parts of the screen.

So, besides having to create keyboard mapping templates for users so that they would know which keys became which, we would also have to create some kind of label to tell them which keystroke combinations would switch from the bottom of the screen to the top, and vice-versa. In short, it appeared that just teaching the keyboard to our users was going to take a significant amount of time.

The loss of graphic capabilities was not an immediate problem. However, it was an additional factor in our decision to re-examine the future of the terminal emulation approach. Microsoft Windows was beginning to assert itself as a viable alternative to plain DOS, and CD-ROM producers were starting to offer products with some advanced graphics capabilities. Terminal emulation would effectively lock us out of what looked to be the next big wave in the marketplace.

We also began to question the wisdom of so many layers of emulation. To use a Macintosh to get to the CD-ROM meant that it had to emulate a VT-100 terminal to get to the VAX that was using another level of emulation to pretend it was a PC. A certain amount of absurdity became evident in using a PC to emulate a VAX terminal to get to a VAX that is in turn merely emulating a PC.

We wondered too, about the long-range viability of CD-ROM itself as a means of data distribution. Factors such as the plummeting cost of magnetic data storage, and the rise of more Internet-accessible databases, made us consider the possibility that CD-ROM might yet become the "eight-track tape" of the database world. The dedicated hardware and complex layers of software required by these vendor's products would never be usable for anything but CD-ROM. They would all be a dead loss for us if CD-ROM were to lose its viability as a platform for distributed library database access.

Further, VAX/VMS is not a particularly widespread platform at BBN, and we felt that this type of gateway/emulation solution was tying us too permanently to that operating system. Any VAX-based, terminal emulation solution looked like it would have a much shorter life-expectancy than we had hoped.

Additionally, it seemed somewhat self-defeating to reduce the capabilities of advanced machines to the level of a VT-100. Why have all the additional features of a modern desktop computer, if you're just going to pretend it's a dumb terminal?

Finally, cost was a big issue for these two products. Initial pricing for either product in our particular setting was in the $40,000-50,000 range. Our entire project budget was in that same range, which meant we would either have to fight for more money to actually put any databases on this hardware, or find a cheaper way to do things.

Second Phase

Genuine Multi-Platform Access

Dissatisfaction with the terminal emulation solution, both technically and financially, meant a reexamination of our goals. We hoped to provide our users with high-quality access that would use the capabilities of whatever type of machine they had on their desks.

We still had the problem of making Macintoshes read the search software on CD-ROMs written for DOS. At this stage in the project, we briefly investigated a more sophisticated form of emulation than simple VT-100.

There are several software packages available which allow Macintosh users to create a DOS window on their desktops. They can then open any DOS application in that window and run it as if they were using a DOS machine.

We had run the Computer Select database on a standalone Macintosh in this fashion with acceptable results. We decided to try running an emulation program from the CD-ROM server in hopes that our Mac users could run any CD's we chose to mount without having to worry about what platform the search engine was written for.

Given large amounts of RAM necessary for most CD-ROM applications, we were quite apprehensive when we discovered that the product we wanted to use did not support any memory managers. Many of our users' older Macintoshes would not have enough memory available to run our CD-ROMs this way. Further, the client software for the emulator would need to be installed on each Macintosh wanting access to the CD's. At a cost of several hundred dollars per Macintosh for over one thousand potential users, we simply couldn't afford it.

In any event, this type of emulation did not work over our network. There were problems in the way it handled Novell's network drivers, memory management, and BBN's particular Novell server configuration.

When our last flirtation with DOS emulation failed, we committed ourselves to purchasing databases that had multiple-platform search engines available. This would eliminate the keyboard mapping and 24/25 line screen problems that had been such a drawback to terminal emulation. It has, however, proven rather difficult to do in practice, particularly from the collection development perspective. Vendor policies and technical limitations have forced us to take several different approaches to provide the mix of databases our users need.

Our overall goal was now to provide "native mode" access to both Macs and PCs. We could then avoid teaching Mac users a PC interface and vice-versa, and concentrate instead on teaching people when and how to use a specific database to answer their questions.

This approach offered enough advantages for the end user that it seemed worth pursuing, but of course new problems arose as well. One advantage to pursuing this type of solution was that most of the equipment required could be used for things other than CD-ROMs, had we decided to end the project after its initial phase.

As with most complex projects, we investigated several possibilities simultaneously during the development phase. In our case, we had chosen a solution that could eventually provide both Macintosh and DOS access, and possibly provide UNIX access as well. Since not all these possibilities were available right from the start, we adopted a strategy of gradually rolling out the service as each platform became practicable.

We were also committed to offering the service over the existing corporate Novell network. Since Novell is the dominant network system in desktop computers, it is the network operating system most vendors design their products for first. Further, Novell networks can provide access to multiple platforms simultaneously. Because a Novell network was already in place with an existing server that the Library could use, more of our budget could go to database acquisition than we had originally planned.

Beyond Novell, we needed a way to make the CD-ROM itself readable by the network operating system. For our standalone machines, the Microsoft CD Extensions bridged the gap between the operating system and the CD-ROM. For the network, a product called SCSI Express fulfilled this function.

SCSI Express allows a CD-ROM to be loaded as a volume on a Novell network. This means that any machine connected to that network can then see that volume as a drive and can access its file structure. It does not mean that any machine can run any application found on that volume. If an application was written for a different platform it may be visible, but it will not be usable. You still must have a version of the search software for each platform you intend to serve.

Access for DOS Machines

Given our client base, we had originally planned to offer Macintosh access first, then follow with access for DOS users. However, unanticipated difficulties with SCSI Express' beta version of Macintosh access precluded doing things in that order.

Therefore, we decided instead to bring the service up for DOS machines first. Since the CD's were all based on this platform, there would be no cross-platform issues. Temporarily setting aside Mac access meant we were able to get the full production version of SCSI Express and offer immediate DOS access. We could then continue with the Mac side of things when that version of SCSI Express was commercially released.

Starting with DOS users not only gave us a chance to say we had something up and running early on, but provided a test group for trouble shooting purposes. Once they were up we could build on that experience and devote all our time to the Mac client-base. Finally, we could then work on a way to get access to the UNIX users as well.

Since DOS is a minority platform at BBN, we decided that we should install public access workstations in all libraries and reading rooms for those who would otherwise have no access. We originally hoped that we could use 286-class machines to do this. However, the memory overhead required by the network, combined with the large amounts of RAM required by most CD-ROM applications made this impracticable.

To provide public access workstations, we were forced to purchase three new PCs. We did so with some of the money we saved by not having to buy a new server and bought three 486/DX50-class machines.

It seems endemic within CD-ROM applications that the search engine requires enormous amounts of conventional memory. This makes their use over networks more problematic than it need otherwise be. We found that no DOS machine can run the networking software and the CD-ROM software without the use of a good memory manager.

Once the CD-ROMs were up and running for DOS, we planned a lunchtime rollout demonstration in the company auditorium. This was announced to the company as a whole through readily accessible channels such as electronic mailing lists, corporate library newsletters, posters, and word-of-mouth.

We focused the demonstration on how to use the databases effectively, rather than on the technical details of access to the Novell network. Most of the presentation discussed what types of data were available, when to use which database, and what kinds of results one could expect. The session also included handouts with details instructions on the means of connecting to the databases.

With the DOS side of things now in place, we could concentrate entirely on making things available to our Macintosh users.

Access for Macintoshes

Since most of the BBN staff use the Macintosh platform, this part of the project was in many respects the most important one. It was also extremely problematic for many reasons.

SCSI Express, which we needed to make the CD-ROMs readable by Macintoshes, proved initially problematic on the Mac platform. The vendor, Micro Design International, had promised us Macintosh access from our first contact with them, but the beta version of the product created some unexpected difficulties under our configuration. Most importantly, it seemed to make our Novell server extremely unstable. Since the server was needed by more departments than just the Library, and the vendor needed some time to investigate the problem, we backtracked to a more stable DOS-only version of the product, as mentioned above. A further irritation was that the production date for the Macintosh-supporting version was delayed from initial estimates of December 1992 to an actual release date of spring 1993.

Ideally, we hoped each application would have a DOS and a Macintosh search engine resident on the disc so that when a user opened the application, the appropriate search software would start. This was not often the case.

Of our initial networked databases, only Disclosure worked this way, making it the easiest product to bring up. Once the DOS version was up and running, we could add the Mac users as soon as SCSI Express allowed access to that platform.

During this stage of the project, Computer Select provided us with a beta Macintosh version of their database. We found it not fully developed enough for our use however. Therefore, we continued with their DOS version until a full production version for the Macintosh shipped. At that point we were able to bring this product up for our Mac-based users. However, the vendor licenses this particular product by platform and number of users rather than simply by concurrent users. This forced us to discontinue its network availability for our DOS users.

Our existing database of business literature, in common with most vendors, did not offer a Macintosh version of their product. In fact, we could not find any general business database at that time that offered a Macintosh version. Since the initial phase of the project served only DOS users, we decided to network this database as an interim product. It was a particularly attractive option since they did not charge a fee for a network license.

As this phase of the project came to a close, we planned a repeat of our lunchtime auditorium demonstration for all those products we were now making available to our Mac users. This session was simply a modification of our initial session, incorporating any necessary differences for the Macintosh platform. We also conducted tutorial sessions for several senior executives to promote their use of the new service.

Hardware & Software Costs for the Project

Our total budget for the first year of the project was estimated at $40,000. Recall that network licenses and database subscriptions cost us about $23,400.

Rather than purchasing a new network server, we purchased only the necessary SCSI adapter and CD-ROM players, attaching them to a server purchased by the PC Support group. Had we attempted to do the project strictly from within the library's budget, the cost of the server would have greatly restricted the number of databases we would have been able to network.

The total expense for the hardware and software the Library needed to run the project came to approximately $17,000. With the database costs mentioned above, this brought the library share of the project total to $40,400, which was on target with our initial estimates. Adding in the cost of the server bought by the PC Support department brought the total to approximately $65,400.

The VT-100 emulation solution we had originally planned, would have cost between $70,000 and $80,000, somewhat above what even our combined resources could have accommodated.

Continuing the Project

Changes to Database Offerings

Immediately on the heels of the Macintosh rollout in the spring of 1993, we began to re-examine which databases we offered on the network. Our fiscal year runs from July 1 to June 30, and the Library would assume all database renewal costs in the coming year. We changed and expanded our offerings in several ways.

The new products we were most happy with were from Dialog OnDisc. This search engine comes in both Macintosh and DOS versions on all of their CDs. It's essentially the same search software, (allowing of course for differences in the way the data in the file is structured), as that for Disclosure/SEC, with which most of our users were already familiar. A further advantage for the Library's professional searchers is the ability to search using the Dialog command language.

We added subscriptions to the Boston Globe and ERIC from Dialog. Both were relatively trouble free to bring up and both receive regular use. ERIC is a bibliographic database covering research in education. It provides an important resource for our educational technology department. *The Boston Globe* is of obvious general applicability.

We were unhappy that one of our most popular databases, Computer Select, was still inaccessible to our Macintosh-based clientele. When we got the news that they were finally shipping a production version of the database for the Mac, we were quite excited.

Unfortunately, the Macintosh version proved to have none of the sophisticated field searching capabilities of the DOS product. Although the vendor has promised that this will change, the Macintosh version has not yet added field searching capabilities.

Nor were we pleased to learn that licensing was by platform plus number of concurrent users. This meant that to continue offering this database to both sets of users we would have to pay for two network licenses, and dedicate two CD players for just one set of data. In the end, we switched our networked subscription to the Macintosh version because of the balance of our client base, but retained a standalone subscription of the superior DOS/Windows version for more precise searching use in the Library. This of course, somewhat defeated the purpose of networking the database to begin with, but we simply could not afford to run two entirely separate subscriptions to this database.

The DOS-only general business database we began the project with was replaced by one that offered access to both platforms, F&S Index Plus Text, from the Information Access Company. This product uses Silver Platter Inc.'s SPIRS search software, which runs under both the DOS and Macintosh platforms. The advantage of a dual platform search engine combined with the excellent Predicasts coding system, made this change very obvious and easy for us.

While this product has received greater use then its DOS-only predecessor, it has not been without its drawbacks. Chief among them are the inability to run the Macintosh version of the database directly off the server, which means that every user needs to have hard disk space available to install the search software on the desktop. Also, since the volume name on the disk changes each month, and the software won't allow you to change that name back to a standardized name, all the batch files and Macintosh aliases which call the database by its volume name must be changed every month. This has been very irritating for our patrons, who are forced to download a new copy of the alias each month. They angrily remind us of this inconvenience with great regularity, but we have not yet found a solution to the problem.

Changes to Costs

Annual database licensing and subscription costs for the revised configuration increased, since the success of the initial phase had created a demand for more databases. We increased the number of databases offered over the network by a third, while increasing our subscription costs only 23%. The coming fiscal year will probably see a few other changes as well as we try to improve the usefulness of what we make available.

Expanding Services to UNIX Users

As mentioned previously, there are very few commercial CD-ROM databases available in UNIX versions. Therefore, we have investigated various other approaches to provide access for the BBN UNIX community. All these choices involve terminal emulation in some form, and are therefore less than ideal.

Recall that the two major problems we found with terminal emulation are keyboard mapping and screen size. These problems are still with us as we search for a solution for UNIX users.

The first approach we investigated was to set up a PC as a telnet client. A networked PC would wait for a UNIX computer to connect to it, then send copies of its screens to the UNIX computer. The problem was that since MS-DOS can only perform one task at a time, it could only provide access for one UNIX user at a time. This was obviously unacceptable.

A further problem with the telnet approach was that it assumes a 24-line screen. This re-created the same screen size problems that caused us to reject the terminal emulation approach mentioned above.

Therefore we decided a preferable approach would be to use a UNIX technology called X Windows. X Windows can provide any size screen the UNIX user desires, so that while the keyboard mapping issues would remain a problem, we could eliminate all of the screen size issues.

After some investigation, we identified a product that places a version of the X Windows operating system on top of MS-DOS instead of Microsoft Windows. The vendor assured us it would provide multi-tasking so that multiple UNIX users could reach the PC simultaneously using X Windows. Unfortunately, in practice we could not get this feature to work. Other users on the CDROMLAN discussion list experienced similar problems.

Abandoning that approach, we developed another. Our current approach, not yet tested, is to install a PC-based version of the UNIX operating system that accepts X Windows connections from other UNIX computers. This version of PC UNIX can run multiple "virtual" PCs on the same machine, which means that multiple UNIX users could then access it simultaneously. Our hope is that a UNIX user will be able to open an X Window that provides a 25-line MS-DOS screen, launch and use a DOS-based CD-ROM, and close down the that specific "virtual" PC session when the search is complete.

Conclusions

This type of project requires the expertise of both library and computer support staff. Either department attempting to do this project alone would have had a great deal more difficulty, resulting in much higher costs and far greater expenditure of time. Working together, we developed a new and important corporate resource that is well thought through and well managed. Just as database selection and search training benefit from a librarian's expertise, so too, does the network benefit greatly from being professionally managed by the computer support staff. Splitting the costs between departments also meant that the scope of the entire project could be that much larger.

From the library point of view, this project made important library resources much more visible, provided a readily acceptable tool for teaching basic searching concepts, gave the librarians an important "showcase" for their professional search skills, and made the library generally that much more valuable to the company.

From the computer support point of view, it added a highly visible corporate resource to their list of supported products. Using the library staff as a group of trained promoters and trainers lightened the training burden on the PC support group. They also broadened their expertise by adding an additional technology to the types of products they support. Finally, it furthered their ongoing goal for greater centralization of computer services within the corporation.

Both departments have benefited from the closer relationship by finding other projects to exploit their mutual interests. The trust we developed between the two departments has continued to bear fruit, particularly as we look at new ways of improving accessibility to resources and tools available over the Internet.

Our decision to work with CD-ROMs that could provide native mode access to both the Mac and the PC platforms, while increasing the difficulties for collection development, nonetheless means we can provide a much more sophisticated level of access to the databases than would ever have been possible under terminal emulation. While we will still be confronted with some terminal emulation issues as we expand our services to the UNIX platform, the great flexibility of that operating system gives us a reasonable expectation of near-native mode access to those users as well.

BIBLIOGRAPHY

CDROM-L. [Online]. Available e-mail: CDROM-L@uccvma.ucop.edu.

CDROMLAN. [Online]. Available e-mail: CDROMLAN@idbsu.idbsu.edu.

Akeroyd, J. "CD-ROM networking." *Information Services & Use* v. 12 (n. 1, 1992):55-63.

Akeroyd, John. "CD-ROM networking in practice." In *Computers in Libraries International* 91, pp. 168-172. London, UK: LISA, 1991.

Bucknall, T. and R. Mangrum. "Using Saber Meter and Saber Menu to manage access in a CD-ROM network." *Library Software Review* v. 11 (n. 3, May June 1992):2-7.

Ciufetti, P. "Networking CD-ROMs: practical applications for today and solutions for the future. Part 2." *Online Libraries and Microcomputers* v. 9 (n. 1, January 1991):1-4.

Ciuffetti, P. "Networking CD-ROMs: practical applications for today and solutions for the future." *CD-Rom Librarian* v. 6 (n. 11, December 1991):12-17.

Francis, E. "Mainframe compact disc networking at Glaxo Inc." *CD-Rom Librarian* v. 7 (n. 4, April 1992):12-15.

Heinisch, C. "CD-ROM-retrieval in heterogeneous networks conceptions, solutions, conclusions and influence on library management." In *Information Technology and Library Management*, 13th International Symposium, pp. 115-36. Essen, Germany: Universitatsbibliothek Essen, 1991.

_____. "Networking CD-ROM in German libraries." *CD-Rom Librarian* v. 6 (n. 11, December 1991):21.

Johnson, D. "CD-ROM selection and acquisition in a network environment." *Computers in Libraries* v. 11 (n. 9, October 1991):17-22.

Ka-Neng Au, . "Hardware options: from LANs to WANs." *CD-Rom Librarian* v. 7 (n. 3, March 1992):12-18.

Kittle, P.W. "Networking the light fantastic-CD-ROMs on LANs." *CD-ROM Professional* v. 5 (n. 1, January 1992):30-1, 33-4, 36-7.

Koren, J. "Multiuser access to CD-ROM drives without a CD-ROM LAN. I." *CD-ROM Professional* v. 5 (n. 4, July 1992):59, 61-4, 66.

_____. "Providing access to CD-ROM databases in a campus setting. II. Networking CD-ROMs via a LAN." *CD-ROM Professional* v. 5 (n. 5, September 1992):83-4, 86, 88-9, 91-2, 94.

Kratzert, M.Y. "Installation of a CD-ROM local area network: the untold story." In Proceedings of the 12th National Online Meeting, pp. 201- 7. Medford, NJ: Learned Information, 1991.

Kriz, H.M., N. Jain and E.A. Armstrong. "An environmental approach to CD-ROM networking using off-the-shelf components." *CD-ROM Professional* v. 4 (n. 4, July 1991):24-31.

Lee, R.B. and L.B. Balthazar. "The evolution and installation of an in-house CD-ROM LAN." *Bulletin of the Medical Library Association* v. 79 (n. 1, January 1991):63-5.

McQueen, H. "Fundamentals of LAN/WAN access to CD-ROM and alternative information technologies." Quarterly Bulletin of the International Association of Agricultural Librarians and Documentalists v. 37 (n. 1-2, 1992):89-90.

Paul, D., J. Latham, K. Mitchell and J. Nikirk. "The over-the-counter CD-ROM network solution." *CD-Rom Librarian* v. 6 (n. 9, October 1991):19-23.

Rao, S.N. "The implementation of high-tech reference services in a medium-size academic library." *CD-Rom Librarian* v. 6 (n. 11, December 1991): 18-20.

Sloan, S. "The ABCs of networking CD-ROMs. 26 depressing reasons why this may cost you more money than you think." *CD-ROM Professional* v. 4 (n. 1, January 1991):29.

Winterman, V. "CD-ROM networking: an overview." *Library Micromation News* (September 1991):7-10.

Chapter 15
The BP Nutrition Virtual Library: A Case Study

Michel Bauwens

The following study is divided into four parts. It starts with a short description of the specific information needs of a group of senior managers within a large multinational company. The second part describes how the sole Information Officer operated a "virtual library" to fulfill these needs. The third part discusses the uses of information refinery software that was instrumental in achieving our goals. Finally, it concludes by looking at the implications of our experience for a wider corporate and professional environment, and the justification for a new organizational model.

The Information Needs of Senior Management

BP Nutrition (BPN), at the time the virtual library was in operation, was one of the four divisions of British Petroleum (the others being Oil, Chemicals, and Exploration), and consisted of about 200 operating companies, organized in nine business groups, with a staff of almost 25,000 and a $5 billion annual turnover. The rather "lean" worldwide headquarters of this animal feed group was located in Antwerp, Belgium, and consisted of 20 senior managers and support staff (ten secretaries, five professionals). The headquarters originally had been located in London where its information needs were supported by a traditional library operated by four librarians. The move to Antwerp meant a move for the physical library but not for its staff, who remained in London until the information services were drastically downsized. BPN management in Antwerp therefore hired one Information Officer with the charge to operate the library and fulfill the information needs.

What were these needs? First of all, senior management wanted to monitor the activities of its competitors, a mix of about twenty multinational organizations (MNOs) from the agribusiness and food processing sectors. Second, they required an intimate knowledge of the markets they operated in (animal feed, processed meat, animal breeding, etc.). Third came all developments in the business and regulatory environment which could have an impact on the company. These concerned not only issues such as the European Union's Common Agricultural Policy and GATT negotiations, but also the public's mood on issues such as waste management, biotechnology, and the like.

Such information has to be current and needs to be delivered fast. People need tomorrow's information yesterday. Coverage has to be both comprehensive and selective. The information needs to be as high as possible on the value chain. Thus, we distinguished raw data, organized information, knowledge (information digested into the current knowledge base), intelligence (when the acquired knowledge is applied to action alternatives), and the elusive wisdom, a state of awareness when there is no longer a gap between one's actions and the accumulated intelligence. In other

159

words, senior management would certainly not be satisfied with merely a list of bibliographic references. Usability was also a critical factor in the sense that the information delivered should be integrated into the existing work-flow and that the necessity for retyping should be kept to a minimum. Very important is the "readability" factor, which means that desktop publishing is no longer a luxury, but a sine qua non requirement. Information products should be visually attractive!

The information center operates under a number of political and economic constraints as well. It is usually considered an overhead cost and therefore repeatedly in the line of fire at a time of downsizing and recession. During the period 1990-1993 overall staff levels at BP were reduced 15 percent, but the information staff lost more than 90 percent of its members, going from 300 to less than 15 worldwide. Furthermore, we are operating in the context of "infosiege." There is a growing perception that there is too much information and that protective filters are necessary.

It became clear to the Information Officer that being a one-man-band would mean that it was impossible to deliver an efficient service using the traditional methods. Was it really necessary to maintain a physical library which was used only occasionally, yet necessitated a good chunk in administrative working time? Was it really necessary to build collections of material which was also available outside? My answer was negative. I took perhaps the bold step of abolishing the paper library altogether, focusing on the efficient use of electronic resources, coupled with rapid document delivery on the basis of need. Before we describe these working practices, it is useful to compare the notion of the traditional paper-based centralized library with the emergent concept of the virtual library. I realize that in practice most readers will encounter mixed library systems where automation has been implemented incrementally, but I believe we are really faced with two paradigms or "ways of seeing the world."

The Virtual Library and Theory and Practice

The traditional library is a centralized paper-based resource, a place consisting of books and periodicals, to which the customers need to transport themselves physically in order to receive a service. This centralized organizational model has a number of drawbacks. For instance, information requests usually arrive through a number of middlemen; hence queries are distorted. It also ensures that it is these middlemen, usually middle managers or junior assistants, who will receive the credit for the work done, leaving the library in a politically weak position. Such a library is, by definition, limited to its physical collection. The fact of having several librarians in the same location has advantages but also drawbacks. One's colleagues become fellow librarians, and not the experts or other customers from the staff. This may lead to skewed vision as far as priorities are concerned.

The virtual library is in the first place a service, and because it is not bound to any location, it fits into a networked organizational model, with direct electronic links to all potential customers, which cuts across hierarchical boundaries. Its resources are potentially unlimited. The vast and growing array of electronic resources, which can be accessed through telecommunication links with a PC and a modem, are part of its potential collection. Simplified to the extreme, it could be said that all the information everywhere in the world can be accessed from anywhere and sent wherever the customers are. The librarians staffing such a virtual library are extremely flexible, can be integrated into any physical or virtual work-team, and are therefore "outward bound." Their colleagues are the other experts of the organization.

The traditional library is labor-intensive (indexing and cataloguing activities, etc.) and hence both slow and expensive in terms of man-hours. The virtual library is technology-intensive, hence speedy, but cheap in man-hours. A very important distinction is the acquisition philosophy of both models. The first focuses on just-in-case collection building, though certain studies have shown that no more than 20 percent of such a physical collection will be used at least once. The virtual library focuses on access and the just-in-time delivery model.

The BPN approach was based on the above description of such a virtual library model in certain specific ways. Thus the paper collection was abandoned in favor of an exclusive reliance on electronic resources, coupled with rapid document delivery of the items identified in that way, in case the primary documents were not available online. We did not have the means to digitize the primary material, as it became clear that our plans to use document imaging had to be shelved because of the managed exit strategy of British Petroleum. Our parent company indeed decided to leave its agribusiness activities for 1994. We therefore admit that we should properly speak about a "garage" version of a virtual library, because of the incomplete digitization of the process. We do not use the term electronic library though, as we think that such a term should be applied to the electronic equivalent of a paper library, i.e., a limited collection exploited from a particular perspective and organized in a particular way that enhances accessibility for a specific group of users. The BPN virtual library simply relied on the efforts of external information providers and accessed these on their terms.

BPN did not rely only on electricity, however; it also complemented its information strategy with human bonding techniques. Thus, the customer was king and direct contact with requestors was always favored. A deliberate effort was made to be integrated into working teams to make the information process interactive.

The problem of adding value was addressed in a particular way. In my view the information professional has his own core competence which centers around the retrieval and delivery of information as well as the management of the whole process. However, can we compete with the subject experts such as the financial analyst or the marketing specialist? I do not believe we generally do, and hence advocate a teamwork approach whereby it is those particular experts who add value, though of course the librarian should manage and preferably formalize this process. I do believe our expertise is crucial though and hence we are knowledge workers. This means all routine procedures should be banned as much as possible, either through automation or outsourcing.

We will now describe these working practices in terms of hardware, software, infoware and peopleware.

Hardware

The hardware requirements are minimal, consisting of a personal computer, a modem, and access to telecommunication links.

It is important to realize what can be done without leaving our desktops. In BPN we had access to the appropriate internal and external e-mail networks. Sending faxes and telexes could be done in such a manner as well, for instance Data-Mail. Fax modems offer even more possibilities. Services such as MCI Mail even allow us to send postal mail, which is then remotely printed close to the place of delivery. If we apply such a working practice in a consistent way, the advantages are obvious. First, one achieves professional independence from secretarial support and avoids being hindered by telephone tag, postal delays, and lining up at the fax machine. Being a One-man-band is transformed from a limitation to a very efficient proposition.

Crucial here is the "seamless web" factor which avoids any information bottleneck. Consider this not infrequent scenario: while at work in a word processing document, a beep informs me of an incoming electronic mail message which is promptly read. After some thought is given to the appropriate sources and search strategy, an online query is undertaken and the results downloaded, preferably in a format compatible with the customer's PC package (a Lotus spreadsheet for example). After some editing, the electronic document is sent to the requester, who is also alerted and can immediately start working in his PC. No bottlenecks and paper have intervened in the process to inhibit the rapid flow of information.

Infoware

We begin our review of information sources with the traditional databases. More than 8,000 of them are available worldwide. The BPN information center had access to about 1,000 databases through ten hosts. These were used to respond to ad hoc queries and to generate current awareness services.

Using SDIs was a very important part of our information strategy. Readers will be familiar with the procedure whereby database updates are matched with an interest profile, and the relevant items are then sent to an electronic mailbox. Such an environmental scanning is important to offset the loss of proactivity inherent in the just-in-case acquisition policy that we abandoned. The justification of the latter is that a librarian can anticipate the needs of his users, even though we know that a majority of acquired items will never be used at all. Through an effective SDI policy we compensate for this loss by sending a comprehensive series of pointers, leaving the user to decide whether he wants to pursue certain matters.

Comprehensiveness is very important. The user has to feel that the business environment is well monitored, and that he can safely abandon scanning a variety of just-in-case paper journals. Thus it is not sufficient to generate one alert from one database for one user. It is necessary to use a wide variety of database sources, in order to produce customized products (i.e., just-for-you publishing). An intimate knowledge of the user's needs has to be translated in an information map which shows how different sources join in the particular stream appropriate for that particular user. This can reach a level of detail whereby one identifies which database uniquely covers an important periodical.

At BPN, the general and trade press was monitored through Textline, the FT Profile newsgroups, and Promt, all strong on international coverage. These were supplemented with databases that showed a regional bias, such as Infomat (Europe), Delphes (France), and Asia-Pacific. Some of these databases are not available through hosts (Informatie Bank en Infotrade for Dutch and Belgian material). MAID was used to generate TOC-SDIs in agribusiness and management. Newsnet, where the mailbox is updated every fifteen minutes with material from the newswires, was useful to monitor hot topics during crises.

The information professional functions as an information refinery and repackages the source material (with intellectual editing as well) according to the needs of specific customers. This function requires a good knowledge of these users. In BPN all senior managers were originally interviewed for forty-five minutes, and these interest profiles were updated through in-depth information audits (done in-house with the help of MBA interns). These audits were occasionally supplemented by questionnaires to the recipients of specific products. Generally the procedure can be summarized in four steps: (1) information requirements analysis, (2) matching needs to appropriate sources, (3) trial runs and feedback, and (4) automating or outsourcing the process.

To be truly effective such a comprehensive monitoring of the business environment has to be coupled to rapid document delivery whether the primary material is available online or not. Good relationships with document delivery services are crucial and one has to be willing to pay premium prices in cases of urgency. Part of the savings from the switch from just-in-case to just-in-time has to be reinvested in such services. Document delivery replaces collection building for documents that are available through external channels.

The BPN current awareness program produced a wide variety of customized journals. The primary product was a monthly Competitor Alert. Each of the nine business groups, and several strategic business units and working groups, received the appropriate sectoral alerts (French Poultry and Meat, Eastern Europe Agribusiness, for example). Different management functions also received specific products ("Virus Alert" for the Information Technology department, an "HR" alert, etc.). Finally, in cooperation with the Corporate Communications department, a whole program of Issue Management was set up, covering topics such as animal welfare, waste management, biotechnology, etc. It is perhaps good to remind the reader that all these alerting services (twenty-plus, using fifty SDIs as source material) were produced by a solo librarian. This was possible only through the use of the appropriate information refinery software, which will be discussed later, after a review of nondatabase sources. Indeed, databases generally provide only published information, but for in-depth coverage of projects one needs contextual information, for which experts need to be contacted. This is why the other computer communication tools enter the picture.

Electronic mail is the basic technology. Through the Internet, one has access to millions of professionals, linked to the academic, commercial, and social networks. These can be contacted either individually (if confidentiality is important) or collectively by approaching the appropriate bulletin boards or mailing lists. The first are common electronic spaces one has to access deliberately, while the latter are lists of subscribers that will receive each other's messages on a given subject domain. A great advantage is that one avoids telephone tag and can reach many experts in one stroke. They are ideal tools for the typical "does anybody know" queries. Even if such a question does not always yield the complete answer (it rarely does), the "gift economy" so characteristic of the Net will give you useful tips and contacts. The Internet can also be used for networking with colleagues and is a vast resource for purposes of continuous professional development. The network also serves as a giant database with more than two million datafiles available for the asking, and more than eight hundred library OPACs accessible through remote login. BP America devised a cooperative working agreement for joint monitoring of professional mailing lists. CompuServe was used for some experiments in real-time conferencing. Used creatively, these resources are indispensable for a solo librarian who cannot rely on colleagues in physical proximity.

The combination of external databases and network resources (and in-house document imaging and CD-ROMS, which were not used in BPN) leads us to posit a new view of the library professional, who is no longer operating among a stack of books, but in the middle of different layers of cyberspace, a vast ocean of data accessible from his desk. We use the term "cybrarians" for thse librarians who are able to navigate cyberspace.

Peopleware

What kind of manpower is needed to operate such an electronic library? Obviously such an information professional needs some basic computer literacy and online experience. For the added value of the networks, simply add the knowledge of a few basic commands needed to operate electronic mail. If this sounds simple, that's because it is. Interfaces are indeed becoming increasingly user-friendly. More important is the necessity to be well connected to the networks and to have a good variety of databases at one's disposal. Crucial, however, is the availability of information refinery software.

Information Partner

The great problem we were encountering in our production of alerting services was the time-consuming post-processing routines and the time needed to produce the required DTP documents. It took about twenty minutes to edit an alert in a word processing document, and another twenty to publish the newsletter. Indeed all hosts, and even individual databases, have specific formats and structures that need to be streamlined. Also, we needed to redirect items to specific users as well as do some intellectual editing. Overall, we needed to spend at least twelve hours a week (usually more) with these routine tasks, a situation which became untenable.

The acquisition of Information Partner greatly reduced this problem. The software is a combination of communications software, text processing, and desktop publishing, with the necessary reformatting routines. First, it preprograms and executes searches without human presence. Second, it reformats the incoming data in a consistent format and allows for easy reorganization of the material. For example, it automatically produces table of contents, with subdivisions if required. It adds tags to the records that are recognized by the DTP program, thus producing a high-quality newsletter at the touch of the print button. Overall, post-processing time was reduced by two-thirds. It is possible to produce a DTP-ed newsletter or report in less than seven minutes. Such software is a sample of the kinds of tools we will need even more in the future if we want to pursue our ideal of becoming knowledge workers freed from routine tasks. The saved working time (one day a week!) could be used for further innovation and professional development.

Conclusion

What were the results of the above-described experiment with the virtual library model? First of all, we were able to serve a growing constituency of customers. Starting with top management who used our services intensively, we gradually expanded our work to the nine business groups (who used our services regularly), and finally even to operating companies. An information audit, and the reception of a special award, confirmed the satisfaction of our users. This effort was achieved in the context of a budget that had been reduced by 30 percent three years in a row. My senior managers concluded that the one-man virtual library was more efficient than the previously operating four-man paper library.

We believe our experiment exemplifies an efficient information management model based on the following premises: (1) a great majority of the secondary material (abstracting and indexing services) is available online; (2) the primary material is available online or through a regular document delivery channel although it need not be kept locally; (3) the residue, i.e., added-value printed material not available through these normal channels, should be kept locally but digitized and made available through remote login throughout the organization. (In other words, let's apply the Internet model internally as well.)

Our slogan should be: act locally, benefit globally. Such a global usage easily justifies investment in document imaging. Thus we strongly believe in the following organizing principle: one organization, one networked library, one cyberspace. One organization means that information is the property of the whole corporation, not of the individual or department processing it. One networked library refers to the availability through remote login of this locally produced information. One cyberspace refers to the creation of a common mental space through computer-mediated communication, the creation of an electronic commons that becomes the knowledge base of the organization.

The information professional becomes a cybrarian, i.e., a guide to cyberspace, both the external the and internal spaces. We call this infomapping (a term coined by Woody Horton). Internally, this involves close relationships with internal teams, experts, datafiles, etc. and a role as the institutional memory of a company's knowledge base. Externally it is simply the continuation of our role of providing information or access to it. With the growth of end users, access and guidance will become more important than direct provision. Creating maps to cyberspace will become very important. Think, for example, of the necessity for creating virtual electronic reference libraries in the groupware environment. Outsourcing, or rather outsourcing management, will become increasingly important, and involves the creation of alliances and partnerships with external providers such as information brokers. All these activities presuppose networking, perhaps our foremost role. We will need to be networked inside the company with our colleague-cybrarians and other experts, through professional associations, and of course, through the electronic networks.

Because we will become increasingly location-independent, I advocate a new organizational model, in which the central corporate library is replaced by a network of strategically placed cybrarians, in close physical contact with the users (though it is advisable to retain a small central core as a support unit). Let us use the new technology to be closer to our customers (hot-desking if necessary), rather than to go away from them, such as in teleworking. Alternatively, we could move "virtually" through the groupware environment, where we would be attached as information counsellors to the various and changing virtual teams of our increasingly "virtual corporations" (i.e., constantly adaptable constellations of experts, located throughout the world). It is crucial to reengineer our working practices, in order to take advantage of the new technology, rather than simply to automate our existing practices.

Historically, librarians have been in charge of the physical organization of knowledge (stacks of books brought to the visiting customer), and of its conceptual organization. The first role, a transport role, involves clerical tasks of low added-value. This role can now be carried out with information technology. The second role is a pure knowledge worker's role and becomes increasingly important in an age characterized by an explosion of the amount of information. At BP Nutrition, we eliminated the clerical tasks as much as possible to focus on the second. We believe this to be a way forward for the whole profession.

Chapter 16
Nonprofit Organizations: Opportunity for Information/Library Management
Saralyn Ingram

Consumers Union is a nonprofit organization best known as the publisher of *Consumer Reports* magazine. This paper briefly describes the major functions of the CU library as it strives to meet a unique combination of information needs. Some of the less traditional functions and techniques described may represent opportunities for libraries of other nonprofits to expand their services and increase their value to their organizations.

The Organization — Mission and Background

CU was established in 1936 to provide consumers with information and advice on goods, services, health, and personal finance, and to initiate and cooperate with individual and group efforts to maintain and enhance the quality of life for consumers.

Publications in addition to *Consumer Reports* are *Zillions: Consumer Reports for Kids,* newsletters on health and travel, and books on a wide variety of topics. CU also produces television and radio programs, newspaper columns, and interactive services — Facts by Fax which supplies *Consumer Reports* articles by fax or mail and price services for new and used automobiles. In addition to the printed versions, *Consumer Reports* and the health and travel newsletters are also available online and in CD-ROM format. *Consumer Reports* has also been specially formatted for the Prodigy online service.

Research and testing are pivotal components of CU's work.The Consumer Reports National Testing and Research Center in Yonkers, New York, is the organization's headquarters and home office for 370 of the staff of 420. The Center houses 42 test laboratories and more than 350 offices. The CU staff includes a mix of scientists, engineers, editors, writers, market analysts, survey researchers, lawyers, and experts in many specialities. Most of the nonmanagement employees, professionals included, are unionized and are represented by the Newspaper Guild. The atmosphere is collegial, dynamic, and informal. As with other magazine publishers, the organization is driven by production deadlines.

CU's other offices include those of the Auto Test department and test track in East Haddem, Connecticut, and advocacy offices inWashington, D.C., San Francisco, and Austin. The advocacy office lawyers and CU's Consumer Policy Institute staff testify before federal and state legislative and regulatory bodies, petition government agencies, and file lawsuits on behalf of consumers. Health care reform, insurance, economic discrimination, and the environment are among the recent issues they have addressed.

Income to support these activities is derived from the sale of publications, from small individual contributions, and from a few noncommercial grants. *Consumer Reports*, with a subscription price of $22 per year and circulation of five million, supports much of the work. As a matter of principle, CU does not generate additional income as most publishers do by selling space for advertising in its publications.

The CU Library

The mission of the library is to identify, acquire and provide the business, consumer, and technical information required by CU staff and others to meet management's goals and objectives in a responsive, timely, and cost-effective manner. Organizationally, the library is a department in the Information Services Division. The division also includes the Research and Survey Research departments, which carry out original research, and Reader Service, which answers the majority of reader inquiries.

The library was started in the early years of CU with a file of product standards. Over the years, a myriad of additional functions were assumed, including research, copy-checking, translating, indexing, and current awareness. The archives and records management program are also the responsibility of the library. Opportunities continue to arise for additional expansion of the library's role as it helps CU meet its mission in the rapidly changing consumer media environment.

Library Research

Much library research is related to product testing, the results of which are reported in the pages of *Consumer Reports*. About a hundred categories of products such as hair dryers, motor oil, and refrigerators, in addition to automobiles, are selected for testing each year.

The librarians are an integral part of the team that works on every product-testing project. At the time a project is opened, it is assigned to a market analyst who will help select the product brands and styles that will be tested, the technical project leader who will do the actual testing, the writer and editor who will contribute ideas and write and edit the story, and the librarian who will provide research for the team. In addition to answering any specific needs for information, the librarian provides extensive research files at three points during the life cycle of the project. Each librarian is assigned fifteen to twenty projects at any given time.

Stories based on editorial research rather than product testing cover such topics as supermarket chains, insurance, mutual funds, and nursing homes. Because the information needs for these stories vary greatly, research is not automatically prepared as it is for product stories. Instead the writers request library research based on individual needs.

Other research needs are also handled on an on-demand basis with requests ranging from the very simple, such as an address and telephone number, to more difficult work such as the initial research for a television special on children and advertising. The library has on many occasions alerted requesters that someone else was also working on a particular topic and helped avoid duplication of effort.

Online database searching is a major component of the research function with DIALOG and NEXIS databases being the most heavily accessed. We also use M.A.I.D. (Market Analysis and Information Database) to search market research reports for product sales and brand share and we occasionally access to the CompuServe and Dow Jones services. We are not yet big users of CD-

ROMs but we do find that *Consumer Reports* on disk is very useful at the reference desk. We also subscribe to two CD-ROM services that index product standards—Worldwide Standards Service and DOD Standardization Service—and recently received the NISC Consumer Reference Disc containing *Consumers Index* and *Consumer Health & Nutrition Index*. Most CD-ROM products must come down in price dramatically to be as cost-effective for us as their print counterparts.

Copy-Checking

Although copy-checking is not customarily a library activity, it has been a function of CU's library for as long as anyone can remember. In addition to verifying factual accuracy and reading for clarity and consistency within the stories, the librarians help monitor for consistency in CU policy and position. It is very important to the organization that it speak with a single voice both over time and throughout its multiple publications.

All copy that goes into *Consumer Reports* is checked, as well as all spin-off copy for radio and television scripts, newspaper columns, and press releases. The library also copy-checks the monthly newsletter, *Consumer Reports on Health*, and is checking *Zillions*, and a CU book on a trial basis.

Current Awareness Services

It is critical to the organization that the staff be continually apprised of current events in their many areas of interest and that they be made aware of media coverage of CU's own activities and publications. Therefore, the library established two current awareness services to help meet these needs.

The daily Headline Service provides headlines regarding consumer issues of interest to CU from the *New York Times*, *Washington Post*, *Wall Street Journal* and *Los Angeles Times* via CU's computer e-mail. News Briefs, a newsletter distributed twice a month to the staff, presents excerpts of articles from about fifty periodicals that are scanned regularly. It also includes a brief table of contents of selected foreign consumer affairs periodicals and a list of materials recently added to the library collection.

The routing of periodicals is another way the staff are kept aware of current news in their fields. We subscribe to about 700 periodical titles. Including multiple copies, we receive about 1,030 subscriptions and 980 of these are routed.

Indexing

The library's indexing allows the organization's staff and the people who depend on its publications to quickly retrieve the information they seek. Using Cindex software, the librarian/indexer produces print indexes for four publications: a monthly back-of-the-issue index for *Consumer Reports*, annual print indexes for *Consumer Reports on Health* and *Consumer Reports Travel Letter*, and the index to the annual *Buying Guide*. He also prepares three indexes for in-house use: Last Time Published, a listing of the last time a product was rated in *Consumer Reports,* an index to *Zillions,* and an index to documents produced by CU's advocacy offices. An outside vendor produces and indexes the online product with the library monitoring the indexing. In an effort to improve subject retrieval, a controlled vocabulary was developed in 1992.

High on the library's wish list is a single bibliographic database that would include publications and materials not included on the CD-ROM: *Zillions*, books published by our Books Division, advocacy office documents, and possibly some internal reports. This database would be indexed using the same controlled vocabulary used for the full-text online database. Ideally, then, staff would only have to search this database and the CD-ROM to find all pertinent statements made on a given topic in all Consumers Union publications. This tool would make the copy-checking task of monitoring for consistency much easier.

Translations

Staff frequently request translations or summaries of test articles published in foreign consumer magazines that are *Consumer Reports* counterparts. The library receives about a hundred of these titles and alerts the staff when articles have been published in an area of interest. Translations of foreign product standards are frequently requested and, as the largest member of IOCU (International Organization of Consumer Unions), CU receives letters from around the world that require translating and answering.

Archives

The librarian/archivist provides historical information about the development of the organization, provides access to material for scholarly research, develops exhibits that educate the staff about the consumer movement and CU's history, and contributes stories from the history of CU to the employee newsletter.

The collections in archives include the historic documents of Consumers Union and other selected materials important to the consumer movement in the United States. An extensive collection of photographs that were taken for *Consumer Reports* is available for use by the organization. There are also oral histories and films and a small collection of books that belonged to Colston Warne, a founder and first president of CU.

Materials are added to the archives through the selective acquisition of the papers of leaders of the consumer movement and through CU's records managment program. When the records management program was established, certain records throughout the organization were designated as potentially being of historical interest. When they are no longer needed for current or future business purposes in the departments that generated them, they are forwarded to archives. They are reviewed and all or sections of the documents may be retained permanently in the collections.

Records Management

Each month when the issue of *Consumer Reports* has been prepared for publication, all copy, sources, and other background materials are sent to the library from throughout CU for organizing and storing for future use. All elements of the test project files are recorded in a Paradox database and any missing pieces such as the technical department's "Report to Editorial" are noted and requested. These files are often referred to for future stories and to trace errors in copy as well as for evidence in case of legal action.

When CU planned its move in 1991 from quarters it had occupied for thirty years, the library's role in the management of records grew dramatically — it was asked to develop an organization-wide records program in preparation for the move. A records management consultant and an off-site records storage facility were hired to help with this assignment. Following the move, a more formal, ongoing records management program was developed. The library now works with records coordinators who represent every department or division of the organization. These staff, most of whom are administrative assistants, maintain current records schedules and through the library make use of an off-site facility to store the less active records from their departments.

The library is developing a vital records program that will be part of the organization's new disaster recovery plan.

Financial Issues — The Collection

The selection and budgeting for informational materials in an organization with as many interests and short- and long-term projects as CU has would be extremely difficult if the burden of that responsibility rested solely with the library staff. Luckily, it does not. The library selects and budgets for periodicals, reference services, and other materials of interest to the staff generally or to several departments.

In addition, all CU departments budget for and select periodicals, books, and other informational materials pertinent to their individual interests. The cost of information is also included in budgets developed for each product-testing project. When out-of-pocket expenses, such as those for online database searches, are incurred by the library for research related to product-testing project work or to fill department requests, they are charged to the department or project.

This method of budgeting for and selecting materials allows the people who best know their information requirements to help select materials in their specialized fields. It also allows the library to retain the responsibility for and capability of managing all information resources purchased for the organization, although many of those resources are charged to other budgetary units — the departments and projects. Because the library orders all of the informational materials for the organization, it can prevent the duplication of resources. And by cataloging the books, publicizing newly purchased materials, and routing periodicals purchased by one department to the staff of other departments, the library encourages the organization-wide sharing of resources.

The Library Staff

There are six librarians — four full-time clerks and two part-time employees — on staff, in addition to the library manager. CU's tuition reimbursement policy has helped attract library school students for one of the clerical positions. In addition to support staff duties, this employee backs up the librarians at the reference desk, gaining practical experience for future positions.

Reflecting CU's concern for the disadvantaged, one of the part-timers is a clerk working through a program for disadvantaged high school students established with the local community. CU also organizes a summer work program each year, hiring twenty or so college students, including several who are relatives of employees. The library usually has special projects for one or two of these students.

Not surprisingly, the major cost of CU's library is for the staff. Currently, staff costs are considered overhead although there has been some consideration of allocating this cost to individual departments based on their use of the service. Therefore, for planning purposes and in anticipation that staff that staff costs may be allocated, the librarians track their time by function and the number of research requests by department is tallied.

Librarian Staff Time

Each of the six professional librarians does research, covers the reference desk, and checks copy. Each also has an area of individual responsibility such as archives, records management, or indexing. During a recent twelve-month period, their time was divided among the major library functions as shown below:

Function	Work Hours	Percentage Work Hours
Research	4,159	45%
Copy-Checking	1,620	18
Current Awareness	1,049	11
Indexing	768	8
Collection Developing	359	4
Archives	274	3
Records Management	109	1
Administration	413	4
Meetings, etc.	488	5
Total Work Hours, Clerical Staff Time	9,238	99%

With the high proportion of professionals to support personnel (seven to four) on the staff, it was essential to shift to the computer some of the mundane, repetitious tasks, allowing the clerks to be more productive and expand their roles. The subscription and acquisition functions were automated five years ago with DataTrek software. More recently the circulation system was developed using Paradox database software.

Through our membership in WALDO (Westchester Academic Director's Organization), a library consortium that encourages resource sharing among members, our interlibrary loan function has become faster and smoother. WALDO's members share an online "union" catalog of their book collections and will soon have the capability to request faxes of periodical articles online.

Although our card catalog has not yet been automated, that is the next automation project.

Conclusion

The traditional library functions of collection development and research are extremely important to Consumers Union. Other, less typical, responsibilities such as copy-checking, archives, and records management have expanded the role of the library and increased its value to the organization. The library can become a more valuable asset to a nonprofit organization through the assumption of additonal functions and through:

- *Teamwork.* By including professional librarians as part of a project team when research is a component of the team's work.
- *Monitoring for consistency.* By including copy-checking as a library function in a publishing environment to monitor the consistency of viewpoints expressed in published statements.
- *Chargeback of library expenses.* By charging the cost of library services back to the appropriate cost center, senior management obtains a more accurate analysis of the true cost of its various publications, products, and services and can more readily identify which are valuable to its clients. Charging back avoids hiding expenses, helps establish the true market value of various products and services, and facilitates strategic planning by giving top management more reliable information for better decision-making and financial projections. By continually evaluating current functions and by improving the use of staff time, the department's most expensive resource, the CU Library will be prepared to take advantage of new opportunities to help this nonprofit organization achieve its mission.

Chapter 17
Information Management and the Trade Association
Joan Gervino

A trade association information center plays a unique role within its organization. Ideally the center acts as a clearing house to manage the collection of information within the association, coordinate the flow of inquiries, and assure that the information needs of the members, the association staff, and all of its various publics are handled efficiently and effectively with the level of excellence of a Michael Jordan.

Specialists among the special libraries, trade association information centers are focused on the key issues of their parent organizations. *The Random House Dictionary of the English Language* defines a trade association as "an association of people or companies in a particular business or trade, organized to promote their common interests." Representation of and for the industry is one of the hallmarks of the trade association and is reflected in the collections and activities of their libraries. The staff and resources of the library exist solely to serve the parent association and the industry it represents.

Trade association information centers can vary widely from the one-person library with a small collection of books, special industry reports, documents, and industry newsletters, to the major trade associations with many staff and a broad array of resources in large information centers. Aside from size, other characteristics distinguish one trade association from the next. Although the variations are both intricate and numerous, this article will portray association libraries and information centers as a single genre, highlighting the characteristic key functions and organizational structures.

Traditional Library Services

Trade association information centers, like their counterparts in corporate institutions, maintain a collection of resources—books, reports, periodicals, government documents, and other data sources—in a variety of formats and media. CD-ROM and other databases, audio and video materials, microforms, clipping files, card files, and photograph collections all may be housed, organized, managed, researched, and retrieved in this type of special library.

The library organizes the materials, provides access to the collections, and offers the usual circulation services, —reference, interlibrary loan, periodicals routing, and copy services. The basic range of services resembles those in any traditional library.

The traditional services include all of the internal support functions of serving the needs of the association's staff, including its government relations efforts, which may include maintaining a collection of legislative and regulatory documents, online research services, and other tracking services.

The other characteristics of trade association information centers that differentiate them are discussed in greater detail.

Coordinated Information Management

A key role for trade association information centers is to serve as the clearing house for all the inquiries directed to the association and to organize the information available from the association to facilitate this process. Through the coordination and screening of member inquiries, the information center is able to assure that each caller receives top-quality service.

Placing the association's central switchboard under the information center ensures that all calls are centrally handled through a single information management process. Telephone calls, letters, and any other communications not directed to a specific person or department can be screened and handled by the information center staff, reserving the association's professional staff experts for the specific times when they are needed. This approach also proves useful for filtering nonmember inquiries and assuring that government agency, press and other special categories of inquiries are distributed to the appropriate department.

Although not all inquiries may actually be answered by the center, by developing indexes to all information sources, including in-house experts, the center's staff can be equipped to direct the inquiries where they can best be answered. The right place may be the library or it may be somewhere in the government relations department. Nevertheless, it is the information center staff who screen the inquiries and determine where and how each will get the most appropriate response.

To make the process work effectively, associations need written policies on how inquiries are to be handled, who will be responsible for each category of customer and type of inquiry, and the level of treatment for each.

Easy-to-search text-based PC software that requires little training to manage proves best for organizing resource data that may be needed by the center's information specialists. AskSam (Seaside Software, Perry, Florida) is used by several associations for this purpose.

An important use for data collected about all the inquiries received at the information center is in identifying and planning effective, useful, and responsive services for members, since the information center is in an excellent position to track member needs and wants for information and new products and services.

Centralized information management also benefits the association by assisting in creating a favorable public perception of the industry:

> The trade association library setting provides a unique public relations opportunity for the association and the industry it serves. By providing timely and accurate information, outside interested publics are afforded easy access to information which otherwise might prove difficult to obtain. The library becomes an important additional channel to convey the association/industry message. The apolitical setting of the library serves to enhance the credibility of the message to the public.[1]

Fee Versus Free

The issue of charging nonmembers and even members for access and services from the library has been discussed by association libraries for more than ten years. This is both a philosophical and a bottom line issue.

Some organizations maintain that the information center is one of the key services supported by dues; fees may therefore be offensive to them and avoided completely. Other associations have taken a middle ground, feeling that it is easier and concomitantly supportive of the bottom line to charge only nonmembers; their intent is to ration service to outsiders to conserve valuable resources for the primary constituents, the members.

After researching their library's clientele, some associations have found that only a limited number of members actually utilize the resources offered by the information center. In this scenario, the vast majority of members can view charging fees as a means of shifting one component of an ever increasing dues burden over to the more limited group of members who actually use the information center services.

Increasingly, it is the growing cost of maintaining a library that has convinced association managements and boards that charging fees for services makes sense. For many years at the annual meeting of the Trade and Professional Association Roundtable of SLA's Business and Finance Division, fees for services have remained the number one issue. Indeed, at recent meetings the focus has shifted from *whether* to *how to*, emphasizing new services and opportunities for enhancing revenue generation, with library managers increasingly turning their attention to identifying new product ideas that could become their new *cash cows*.

Strategic Planning Checklist for Evaluating the Fees Decision

As with any new management direction, it is important to be certain that fees for library services will mesh with the overall mission and objectives of the organization. To guide this process, the list of questions below highlights a selection of the strategic issues that should be examined by an association that is weighing the fees versus free decision.

- <u>What is the purpose of the fees?</u> Does the association need to enhance the bottom line? What level of income will be required? How soon will the library be expected to achieve this level? Will fees be imposed simply to restrict the demand for services?
- <u>Are the members involved in the decision-making process?</u> Is this a member or association management decision, or is it driven by the librarian in response to budget constraints?
- <u>Should all services and access be on a fee basis?</u> Do these include loans (rentals), ready reference, on-site use of the library, interlibrary loans, and so on? Most associations have defined fee services as those that are more readily identifiable, are customized for a specific customer, and can be priced without loading on all of the administrative and overhead costs of the organization.
- <u>How should libraries establish prices?</u> Should prices merely be set based on what potential competitors already charge? Do the fees and pricing need to reflect costs and, if so, all direct and indirect costs?

- <u>Are the systems in place to facilitate a fees program?</u> Who will do the billing and record-keeping? Can the accounting department or information center handle the added burden? Will the library be credited with the income or would the funds be lumped with other revenues in a general fund?
- <u>Will the library charge its in-house customers, the association's staff?</u> Does the association have an internal chargeback system, philosophy, and procedures in place for data processing and other in-house services and resources? Is the organization's culture open to this kind of interdepartmental chargeback from the library? Would a chargeback system impose a major burden of record-keeping on an already stretched library staff? Would such a system add to the costs of the organization, because departments would be encouraged to turn to outside sources that might seem to be less expensive, but might cost the organization more overall?

These are just some of the issues that an association needs to address before a fee structure is developed for its services. Going through a strategic planning exercise helps to ensure that any decisions are made for the right reasons and will complement other association goals and objectives.

Variety of Special Services

Association information centers currently offer a diverse and exciting array of products and services beyond the most traditional and universal, such as reference, research, and document delivery. A few of these new and more unusual services are worthy of special mention.

- <u>Electronic communications networks</u> are being operated for their associations by several trade association information centers. These computer-based systems offer electronic mail, daily news services, association-specific information services and resources, product and services ordering, and conference registration, as well as third-party databases (Dialog, Dow Jones News Retrieval, Lexis/Nexis, and Congressional Quarterly, to name a few).
- <u>Conference exhibits</u> enable the library to promote use of the information center, to provide an overview of the breadth of the collection, and to exhibit a range of products available from the library and the entire association.
- <u>The association's archives</u> and other records are managed by many information centers using state-of-the-art technology to assure that all documents and papers are appropriately organized and can be retrieved as needed.
- <u>Clipping services</u> provide their organizations with ready access to both current and historical articles about the association and the industry it represents.
- <u>Database publishing</u>, including both paper-based indexes and online resources, has been developed and maintained by many of the association libraries both to help with their research for responding to member and internal inquiries and as a for-sale service.
- <u>Research reports</u> capturing information from the literature along with possible original research on topics of special interest for the industry serve as a useful resource and an income-generating source for the information center.
- <u>Information kits</u> on a variety of topics and issues are offered by many association libraries. They include articles, chapters of books, other special association materials that can be packaged and offered to members and others at a lower cost than individual, more time-intensive, customized research.

- <u>Publication sales</u> are being handled for the association by a number of libraries in place of a separate customer sales and service center.
- <u>Buyers' guides or consultants' directories</u> have been popular products for information centers. These are designed to include very useful information for members that is not easily accessible elsewhere. Fees can therefore be charged both to the vendors listed and to the recipients of the information.
- <u>Staff resource directories</u> listing all departments, key staff, and phone numbers have been developed at a number of associations. The library staff are familiar with key issues and staff contacts and can compile information for distribution to the membership at large.

Conclusion

The association information center can and should be a key player within the organization. With its knowledge of all the issues and activities within the association's purview and its ready access to vital information and data, the library can serve as a bridge across all departments and concerns and with the membership.

References

1. Steven J. Dorner, director, Industry Information Services, American Gas Association, in Inside Information: *Profiles of Association Libraries and Information Centers*, SLA Research Services #6, compiled by Tobi A. Brimsek. Washington, D.C.: Special Libraries Association, 1991, p. 28.

Bibliography

Gervino, Joan, and Susan M. Hill "Put Information to Work for You," *Association Management*, February 1989, pp. 174-79.

Inside Information; Profiles of Association Libraries and Information Centers SLA Research Series No. 6, compiled by Tobi A. Brimsek. Washington, D.C.: Special Libraries Association, 1991.

Chapter 18
The KPMG Global Information Network
Margaret McClure

The KPMG Global Information Network (GIN) is an evolutionary, worldwide network of information professionals within KPMG. This people network grew out of informal gatherings at professional association meetings beginning in 1978. Today it helps to provide solutions to internal and external clients' international business information problems, and continues to change in response to the demands of business and technological developments. Members have gone from individuals serving single locations to networked participants operating in cyberspace within a global organization. Its growth and development mirror those changes taking place in its parent organization and the general business environment.

KPMG is an international professional services firm formed in 1987 with the merger of Peat Marwick Mitchell and Klynveld Main Goerdeler. In 1993, the firm had 6,100 partners and 76,200 total personnel in Africa, Asia, Europe, the Middle East, North America, and Latin America. It had 1,100 offices located in 125 countries; worldwide fee income was $6.375 billion. KPMG is an umbrella organization for the operating components in each country, each of which has some autonomy. It has an executive office staff in Amsterdam that direct activities such as the development of international standards.

With the vast international merger, research librarians at KPMG foresaw the need to move information across borders quickly and efficiently. Peat Marwick librarians in the United States had been meeting regularly and engaging in informal networking since 1978 through an annual meeting in conjunction with the Special Libraries Association June conference. In the early 1980s, Canadians also started to attend. During the period 1981-1987, joint ventures were initiated, including a directory of information centers and a union list of serials. In 1987 the group decided to conduct an annual meeting separately from the SLA conference.

In October 1989, KPMG information professionals held their first international meeting in Montreal. Several international offices were represented, including Amsterdam, Sydney, and London, as well as fourteen North American offices. At this meeting, the name "Global Information Network" (GIN) was chosen. The group decided to conduct an international meeting every two years beginning in 1990. The Global Information Network, an outgrowth of the informal network created by participation in meetings and ventures, was formed through the initiative of these individuals rather than by a mandate of the firm.

The second international meeting took place in Amsterdam, hosted by Daan Boom of KPMG The Netherlands. Here seven European offices, ten North American offices, and Sydney, Australia, were represented. Members of the Global Information Network decided that they should achieve recognition within the firm, so that they could better serve the organization's needs. To this end, a logo was adopted, and the group embarked upon a structured planning process.

The GIN business plan was developed by a committee consisting of Margaret McClure, KPMG Peat Marwick, Dallas; Lee Fishman, KPMG Peat Marwick, Philadelphia; and Judy Macfarlane, KPMG Canada. Since strategic planning and business planning go hand in hand, the committee first looked at the strategic directions of the firm. They studied the KPMG international mission statement, which emphasizes providing the highest quality of services to clients, building enduring relationships, and being worthy of clients' and society's trust. Other values described are teamwork, innovation, and expertise.

With this background, the committee developed the business plan, articulating the connections between quality information services and the values and goals of KPMG. The message of the plan is that the Global Information Network can maximize quality and efficiency by tapping the resources of information centers worldwide. Each center, headed by an experienced and educated information professional, can also access major public, university, and corporate libraries in its country, along with a variety of databases, national statistics, and other sources. The network serves the firm internally in the delivery of quality services to clients and in business development activities as well as externally in providing information service directly to clients as needed. GIN's motto reads: "We have the people. We have the tools. As a team we can do the job."

The business plan presents information as a commodity, and information storage and retrieval as a business. Information specialists serve as entrepreneurs, operating on a cost-recovery basis for both time and expenses. One valuable information commodity, for example, is competitor intelligence. The writers of the plan wanted the firm to appreciate the resources available from the network. Also, they wanted support for developing information services' mission and resources.

To develop support for the network, its members began an ongoing program of promotional and public relations activities. They first worked on creating and promoting an identity. The name Global Information Network, the logo, the motto, and local promotional brochures all play a part in this effort. The network established responsibilities for its public relations program. The goals of the program are to create a unique identity and market niche, to increase global awareness of GIN's capabilities throughout the Firm, and to get frequent publicity, both within the organization and in the accounting world. Press releases are sent out to appropriate sources. Efforts are made to have an impact at the international level whenever possible. A feature article, "Global Information Network Links Research Capabilities," was published in the KPMG *International Magazine* in March 1990.

The public relations program has an evaluation and follow-up component, so that results can be measured to determine what is effective. One method is to see who does and who does not publish press releases. Another element is to take the items that are published externally, and make sure that they are seen within the firm. Several GIN members were published in their local business press and various trade journals and newsletters. Strategies are reviewed and reworked on a regular basis. Momentum was achieved using a combination of these methods.

Nancy Holland, KPMG Peat Marwick, Washington, D.C., hosted the third international meeting attended by fifteen North Americans, six Europeans, and one Asian. The keynote speaker was Rod McKay, partner-in-charge of National Information Technology Group, KPMG Canada, and member of the KPMG International Technology Committe (ITC). A summary of how and why ITC functions and how GIN should interact with ITC was presented. GIN continues to respond to changes in its environment, both internally and externally. Technology standardization and restructuring of the firm provided new opportunities and challenges. The business plan required revision and new lines of communication needed to be developed with firm and office leaders. Members realized that they need to look for a quick payback on a few ideas, such as worldwide contracts and publishing efforts. The first KPMG Global Information Network Award was presented to UMI/Data Courier for the development of the Accounting and Tax Database.

The telephone is the most frequent method of communication, while facsimile transmission is also used heavily. Electronic mail is good for delivering data files and sending out simultaneously a single message to all information centers within a single country. International use of e-mail had been difficult, because each country has its own electronic mail system. However, this is rapidly changing with developments arising from the Global E-Mail (GEM) pilot project. GIN members were among several select KPMG groups with international communication requirements to be chosen to participate in this project which connects six countries with an easy-to-use interface. Evaluation of user-friendliness, file transfer capabilities, and its effect upon other types of communication techniques followed.

A key benefit that the network offers to KPMG is to place the most advanced research technology at the disposal of the firm's widely dispersed locations. The network enables many centers and information professionals in smaller offices to raise the level of their operation through resource sharing and larger quantity buying power. Common solutions are identifed for the benefit of the firm's bottom line. KPMG is standardizing worldwide on hardware and software to make file transfer easier. Therefore, standardization of library management software is also a high priority. Moreover, GIN can negotiate agreements that allow for local purchasing at attractive rates—an advantage offered to information centers that become part of the network.

The Global Information Network has the *potential* to benefit KPMG in many ways. Information centers in the network can generate significant revenue for the organization, both by billing current clients and by participating in team efforts to win new clients. A wealth of anecdotal evidence exists regarding quality improvements in research products facilitated by drawing upon the local expertise of another information professional in the network. Efficiencies achieved by resource sharing save money for the firm. Early reports indicate that Global E-Mail can cut research time in half. Finally, as mentioned above, money is saved worldwide by negotiating discounts with print and electronic vendors. Melanie Goody, KPMG United Kingdom, achieved success recently with one large database vendor and is working with another for a global contract. Vendors are interested, but have to work within their organizational structure and local/international sales and commission agreements. Some vendors, such as Dialog Information Services, have agreed to regional discounts for North American and European offices only. Matthew Chatterton, KPMG United Kingdom, has carried out a research project on the role and benefits of the KPMG Global Information Network. He is writing a paper that summarizes the progress and results of his investigations to date.

The network continues to develop recognition within the firm. Strategic alliances are forming. The business plan was presented to the International Technology Task Force, a group interested in maximizing effectiveness through information and communication technology. Since such a global information network is a new concept, it is not surprising that acceptance is taking some time. Other factors include the size and the decentralized nature of the Firm as well as varying expectation levels among locations regarding information services. The uncertain business climate in the late 1980s and the early 1990s has also been a consideration. The tremendous effort of the participants, however, has been the key factor in the considerable progress made thus far in this project.

KPMG Global Information Network is quickly becoming a network of cybrarians linked throughout a global organization. In a recent syndicated column, Tom Peters, management guru and advocate of the empowering capabilities of information, praised Michel Bauwens, information officer at BP Nutrition, Antwerp, Belgium, for inventing the term "cybrarian" and for making information widely available throughout his company. Since global coordination adds value to a business, Peters suggests titles such as "Director of Conversations" or "Internal Talk Show Host" and mentions one title in use at McKinsey and Company—"Director of Knowledge Management." He says that librarians, or specifically, cybrarians, are perfect people to fill these roles. GIN is a proactive group of such cybrarians, who manage information, identify relevant electronic and print sources, analyze data, network among experts internal and external to the organization, have technical expertise, understand information highways, and are comfortable in cyberspace.

The Global Information Network is a noteworthy example of information professionals taking the initiative to play an active role in their organization's globalization of operations. The KPMG librarians are using strategic management concepts and the great potential of new technologies to develop their vision into a reality. Over forty KPMG information centers worldwide participate in GIN, and new ones continue to join as members identify other individuals.

- **GIN products**

  (1) Directory of KPMG information centers. The directory contains names and addresses of the centers, names and functions of each staff member, fees charged, languages spoken, and survey of hardware, software, CD-ROMs, and online databases. It is produced on disk as well as in paper format in the Toronto office.
  (2) Union List of Serials, produced in the New York office.
  (3) Procedures manual used in some locations to help ensure standardization among units and to make possible the sharing of solutions.
  (4) Promotional and informational brochures.
  (5) Business Plan.
  (6) Union List of Company Information Sources.

- **GIN programs**

  (1) International meetings of librarians.
  (2) Public relations program.
  (3) Shared information technology and negotiated agreements with vendors.
  (4) Resource sharing and research support.